HOW TO GET THE

---

1 HOUR

REAL ESTATE LOAN

2/3/93

TO DENNIS PALSETTI

— FOR YOUR NEXT REFI!

HOW TO GET THE

---

1 HOUR

REAL ESTATE LOAN

Michael D. Hiller

THE NOTE MODIFICATION AGREEMENT

E & J ENTERPRISES • ENCINO, CA

MERJ Enterprises
16161 Ventura Boulevard, #C-719
Encino, CA 91436, (818) 990-8986

Design by Caroline Poucher/Baron Press

Typesetting by Baron Press

Printed by DELTA LITHOGRAPH CO., Valencia, CA

First Printing — January 1987
Second Printing — May 1987
Third Printing — January 1992

ISBN 0-9618611-0-X

Contents

I have been a lawyer for 25 years. However, I was as intimidated as any of my clients, in obtaining loans on my first small apartment building in 1967.

In dealing with new loans, I was impatient with the burdensome procedures, forms, and rituals—especially waiting for the celebrated approval of the loan application.

You know how frustrating it is to be at the mercy of bureaucracy. They seem to have control over your financial success. The arbitrary and inflexible "formulas" of the lenders are beyond the logic of most borrowers.

You "know" you can pay the loan, if granted.

You can beat this system, under certain conditions, by forcing the big boys to play the game under YOUR rules, after you take away their bargaining chips.

They won't tell you how to get your way.

You will have to disclose that you know how the game is played. Then you demand they play it according to the rules YOU prescribe.

This book will tell you how to take away their advantage of your ignorance of the NOTE MODIFICATION AGREEMENT procedure. You are being given a powerful tool in your financial independence.

The NMA (Note Modification Agreement) will keep you and your investments in the black (and in the pink as well)!

I wasn't born with this information. I had to learn it by experience with lenders. They will cut the red tape when advantageous to them.

You will use the NMA to shortcut their procedures when it is to YOUR benefit.

1

You want to get to the point where you can rewrite your existing loan. You must first familiarize yourself with terminology and tactics which are unknown to the general public. These are kept quiet by big lenders who seek to maximize their bottom line. They won't volunteer information which will allow you to save money, even though you are a good citizen and a credit worthy borrower.

You must also realize that the information on NMAs (Note Modification Agreements) is also kept from most front line employees of the lending institutions. They know only the company way to do business. They have no flexibility in rituals and procedures, going only by the book.

WHAT IS IT THAT THEY ARE KEEPING AS A CLOSELY GUARDED SECRET FROM THE CONSUMER?

Simply stated, there is a way, with the proper case, to get voluntary compliance from your existing lender, to modify your existing note.

You can get market interest rates, those offered by the lender to the general public. You can bypass the SOP, the Standard Operating Procedure, of a four to six month loan processing delay so prevalent in the lending industry.

This tool, which should be mastered by all who want to cut red tape on their current higher interest loan, is the Note Modification Agreement. The NMA gives us the equalizer we need to do battle. It enables us to demand our rights from the multi-billion dollar lender on an equal footing.

No more hat in hand, timidly requesting your loan to be adjusted. You can demand it with the confidence that you are equitably entitled to its benefits, without reservation.

This procedure, the NMA, is laughably simple. Its enemy is the ignorance, obstinance and greed of lenders, The NMA is elementary. It is defined as a contract which modifies an existing Note secured by a Deed of Trust on the subject property—your property.

HOW IS THIS ACCOMPLISHED?

A basic element of contract law is that to be enforceable, the contract must be entered into voluntarily, between consenting adults. Sounds sexy, doesn't it?

The agreement can be, in the case of a leading lender, as short as one page. It basically recites that the original loan terms and Deed of Trust securing the loan remain intact, except as modified in the NMA.

If the original Trust Deed is not replaced by a new one, many wasted and costly procedures are avoided. Most unwary borrowers fall into the trap of a by-the-book refinance with a new 30 year loan. The loan companies have been made excessively wealthy by their use of the SOP. They have done so on the backs of their customers who should be entitled to better and fairer treatment.

Those in the know, which will include YOU who finish this book, have information superior to 90% of the banking, legal and real estate communities. Most who are refinancing their existing loans are blissfully unaware that there is a better mouse trap.

WHAT ARE THE TERMS BEING MODIFIED?

The terms of the loan are of paramount interest to the owner. Obtaining a lower interest rate and monthly payments are the goals.

Obviously, only the borrower can invite a change. You may wonder if this is fair to the lender, based upon interest rate economic realities?

Yes. It doesn't force the existing lender to be in the marketplace. However, if it does offer refinancing to the general public, it MUST give the same benefits to the existing borrower.

The only issues to be decided are:

1. How is it expedited?

2. How much does it cost?

The first question is easily answered by demonstrative evidence. Let the prototype Note Modification Agreement speak for itself in the next Chapter.

2

Form 1 is a simple NMA which does nothing except to change the interest rate and monthly payment on the existing Deed of Trust. All other terms remain the same.

Form 2 is an NMA and SETTLEMENT. It includes a confidentiality clause, waiver of prepayment penalty, one-time assumability, settlement AND NMA.

These forms show how quick and easy it is for the lender to comply with your demands. You avoid the costs, loan application, unnecessary paperwork, delays, excuses given by the lender. Chapter 3 examines the costs of a new loan.

FORM 1- NMA

MODIFICATION OF PROMISSORY NOTE

Loan No. _____

Date: _____

THIS AGREEMENT between EASY STREET SAVINGS AND LOAN ASSOCIATION ("Association"), and
I.M. VICTIM, MAY BEE VICTIM _____ ("Borrower"),

WITNESSETH:

Borrower (or Borrower's predecessor in title) has executed a Promissory Note to the
Association in the original amount of $ 200,000.00   dated October 23, 1981
secured by a Deed of Trust of the same date, recorded in the Office of the County
Recorder of LOS ANGELES   County, California, in Book___3___ , Page_4___ ;
and Instrument Number 81-1023
The unpaid principal balance of said Promissory Note as of this date is $195,000 .

1. IT IS HEREBY MUTUALLY AGREED that said Promissory Note shall be modified in the
the following respect:

    a. Commencing on the___1st___ day of _January__ ,19_87_, interest on the unpaid
    balance shall be at the rate of _10.00__ % per annum.

    b. Commencing on the___1st___day of _February_ , 19_87_ , the monthly install-
    ments of principal and interest shall be $_1,614.28__ and shall be paid on
    ___1st___ day of each month until said principal and interest have been
    paid in full in accordance with· the terms of said Promissory Note.

    c. _____
    _____
    _____

2. If action be instituted on said Promissory Note, I promise to pay the Association
any expenses incurred, including, but not limited to , reasonable attorney's fees
and court costs.

3. In this Agreement the singular shall include the plural and this Agreement shall
be the joint and several obligation of each maker.

4. If any of the provisions of said Promisssory Note conflict with this Agreement, the
provisions of this Agreement shall prevail, but in all other respects said Promissory
Note shall remain in full force and effect.

5. In the event any provision of said Promissory Note or Deed of Trust is held to be
invalid, this shall not invalidate any of the remaining provisions of the Promissory
Note or Deed of Trust.

6. The property described in said Deed of Trust is subject to no encumbrances subsequent
to said Deed of Trust and no one other than the undersigned has any interest in the
property except _____ .

7. Other_____ .

The undersigned consent to this Agreement:

EASY STREET SAVINGS AND LOAN ASSOCIATION

_____ 1/8/87
I. NOTAKRUK Vice-President   Date

_____
I.M. VICTIM

_____
MAY BEE VICTIM

1/6/87
Date
1/6/87
Date

FORM 2- NMA and SETTLEMENT

NOTE MODIFICATION AGREEMENT

Loan Number_____

Date_____

It is hereby agreed by and between EASY STREET SAVINGS AND LOAN
ASSOCIATION, A California Corporation, and the undersigned that
that certain Note date October 23, 1981 secured by a Deed of
Trust dated October 23, 1981, recorded as instrument number
81-1023 said Note being the amount of $200,000.00 is hereby
modified in the following aspects only:

The interest shall be reduced from 13.00% to 10.00% with the
principal and interest payment decreased from $2,214.28 to
$1,614.28 effective with the February 1, 1987 installment.

Privilege is reserved to pay all or any part of the Note at
any time during the term hereof, with no fees nor penalty
whatsoever.

The undersigned also acknowledges a one time assumption of the
loan at the 10.00% interest rate at the time of the assumption
to be allowed to the next buyer of the subject property located
at 888 Rough Road, Los Angeles, California. For all subsequent
sales or transfers, the Association reserves the right to ac-
celerate payment of the Note in accordance with provisions contained in the Deed of Trust.

It is expressly understood and agreed that this Note Modification
is made in settlement of a disputed claim and is not an admission
of liability by any party. It is further understood and agreed
that this Note Modification is confidential in nature and not
to be divulged to other persons or made public in any manner
whatsoever, excluding those persons who have a bona fide interest
in purchasing the subject real property and the heirs, successors
and assigns of trustor, the trustee and its successors and/or
assigns of all or part of the beneficial interest in the Note
and Deed of Trust.

All other terms and conditions contained in said Note shall remain the same.

_____   _____
I.M. VICTIM   MAY BEE VICTIM

EASY STREET SAVINGS AND LOAN ASSOCIATION,
A California Corporation

By:_____
    I. NOTAKRUK, Vice-President

3

Let's examine the usual fees that accompany acquiring a new loan.

The largest is the Loan Fee, usually 1½ % to 2½ % of a new loan principal balance. It is also known as "Points." Each point is 1%.

The credit check and report are paid by the consumer. That's YOU! It can be between ten to twenty times the actual cost to the lender.

The appraisal fee of $250 to $500 is to verify that your property is still in existence. As if an earthquake or demolition has totalled it out!

Escrow fees are paid for document preparation, loan origination. recording of a new Deed of Trust, and $1.00 to $2.00 per thousand of the transaction amount. You can often negotiate the escrow fee downwards. Do it at the beginning of the escrow.

Title check and insurance charges are paid to guarantee that no liens have intervened between the recording of the original and replacement Trust Deeds by the loan company rewriting your loan.

It is also customary to tender a non-refundable application fee of $200 to $500. This entitles you to be given a number to wait in line for funding.

HOW ARE THESE CHARGES JUSTIFIED IF NO NEW MONEY IS REQUESTED?

You are getting the party line about how certain procedures must be utilized to "protect" the lender from losses on bad loans.

Most of us have been taken by this propaganda on past deals and refinancing.

IS THIS COST SCENARIO LOGICAL?

No. It is demanded by conventional and historical procedures.

The bottom line has been the exorbitant costs on the closing statement. The borrower wonders where all the green went.

WHAT WERE YOUR REASONABLE EXPEC-
TATIONS WHEN YOU OBTAINED YOUR
ORIGINAL $200,000, 13% LOAN?

You either were told you could "refinance"
when interest rates went down; OR, it was
implied that you could easily arrange a lower
payment and interest rate by paying new points;
usually one-half of what you paid originally.
You were quoted 1 to 1½ points or that it would
be in the ballpark of assumption fees for a new
buyer. The buyer commonly takes over your
loan for 1% of the loan balance at the time of
loan assumption.

It would have been inconceivable to you,
when you qualified for the original loan at 2
points, that you would be again subjected to the
same rigamarole the second time around.
Nevertheless, your friendly neighborhood
lender requires an appraisal fee of $300, escrow
costs of $2.00 per thousand ($400), miscellaneous closing costs of $500, and $300 title
insurance.

After all, you're not a Johnny-Come-Lately.
Your credit has already been established by
steady, punctual monthly payments. The loan is

permanently on the lender's books until you refinance with a new lender or until you sell your property to a cash-to-new-loan buyer.

At no time did you anticipate, nor should you have, that the lender would demand so-called "garbage fees." They want to fatten their bottom line with unnecessary services which are of no value to you.

Now you are getting the big picture of what the game is. Greed and over-reaching. You are the "mark" in a high stakes, high blood pressure game. You had no inkling you would ever be embroiled in this scene.

HOW CAN THIS GAME BE AVOIDED?

You must have the will power and endurance to make the lender bend to what is logical and reasonable. In so doing, you must first get the company off their arrogance. Expect and demand that they bargain with you in good faith and fair dealing—as an equal.

In law, one-sided non-negotiable agreements are called "Adhesion Contracts." This means that the superior party dictates terms to the detriment of the other party who is in an inferior bargaining position.

This inequality of bargaining position

immediately places you at the lender's mercy. You become vulnerable to the gamesmanship their ivory tower executives have cooked up.

They stick pins in your psyche by non-disclosures and misleading representations. Their entry level personnel are not aware that their promises will not be honored down the road.

You WILL have the tools to win this battle. You CAN beat the banks at their own game. However, you must rewrite the rules—until such time as the Courts of the Legislature do it for you.

4

Having one-sided contracts is such a common-place occurrence that you never think of changing the terms offered. Your choice is limited to taking the least offensive option available.

If you gave it advance thought, you would say: "I'd like these _____ terms. I can get them across the street at CAN-DO S&L.'

"Are you going to give me some incentive to do business with YOU?'

"Incentive" can be spelled different ways: lowered points, free credit check, waiving in-house escrow and document fees, written assurance that you will get the loan, OR refund deposits—if they turn you down.

You can demand disclosure of all terms up-front.

Ask for an estimate of all costs at the time you make your loan application. Get it in writing, before giving up other viable options AND before giving them any non-refundable money.

Giving in to the lender at the beginning leads to sleepless nights. Don't give yourself the added handicap of playing on their turf.

Enjoy what small strategic advantage you have BEFORE making your deal with the lender. After you sign and part with your money, the horse has left the barn!

You let the bank dictate all the terms and you will dance to their tune.

Despite the smiles and geniality you are treated to, your business is as impersonal to them as your social security number.

Do your homework yourself!

Comparison shop. Don't look to your bank for advice! Don't rely on them to tell you the answers.

You are your own best friend. Remember it!

5

You were recently thinking: "How are we going to get out of this mountain of debt?'

"All the interest rates on our own debts are above 11%. Our credit cards are 18%, our Trust Deed is 13%, our car loan is 11%. Our bank accounts pay us only 5%. Our insurance premiums are high.'

"What do we do about our $200,000 loan on the house? It is $6,000 annually above what it should be. The loan company will charge us $10,000 to refinance, if we qualify. Isn't that a joke!!! We can "afford" to pay 13%, but may not qualify to pay 10%!!

"What is this world coming to. We were charged for a credit report to get a lower interest rate despite qualifying 3 years ago for the 13%. Is this standard procedure? They never told us about 'requalifying' when rates went down. They only said it would cost 1-2% to refinance later. They didn't say "Boo" about other fees or other conditions. Gee, I thought our payments proved our good credit.'

"They'd rather deal with a proven track record, wouldn't they?'

"You don't think they are giving us a fast shuffle only to keep our interest rates high? That wouldn't be honest or fair. Isn't there anything we can do about it? If you can't trust your bank, whom can you trust? They were trying so hard to get our autographs that they made promises they couldn't keep. In any event, shouldn't they have to keep their word? After all, it was their goof, not mine."

6

When you first did business with a bank, you enjoyed what you believed to be a close fiduciary and trust relationship. You were paternally guided on loans and financial investments.

Investment counselors were not on every street corner as they are now. Your good relationship with the bank became your security blanket. You had a place to go to get counsel on your money and its best uses.

This old-fashioned banking image has given way to people who are climbing the corporate ladder. In doing so they are stepping on your expectancies. They don't have your best interests at heart.

There are idealistic, honest, and motivated people in banking. However, it is no longer a cut above most other industries, professions, and businesses.

Pressure to perform, to sell loans, to go at a faster pace, permits less attention and less care in dealing with individuals.

Even the highest degree of competence is diminished by greed and ambition. Low competence is covered by a condescending attitude: "Don't bother me with asinine questions. I have bigger fish to fry. Come back later and I'll see if I can squeeze you into my busy schedule." Or, they indicate: "Here is our program. take it or leave it." Or, "Do you understand it (dummy)?"

Inadequacies of the lender's employees are neatly transferred to borrowers. The pervasive feeling given is, "If you were more knowledgeable, you wouldn't need the loan."

However, we all need banks, even though we have to prove we don't need the loan, in order to get it!

7

This book is geared toward doing it yourself.

FIRST, you must have the ammunition to bypass the roadblocks along your highway to the top authority at your friendly lender.

SECOND, you have to be in a positive confidence zone to be able to obtain an NMA. This is important in projecting your visualization into reality. You must taste and feel the NMA as being not only the RIGHT thing—but the ONLY thing you will accept.

You can rely upon support from any source in your battle to achieve equality in the quest for an NMA. It can be Norman Vincent Peale's "The

Power of Positive Thinking," Maxwell Maltz's "Psycho Cybernetics," or your own brand of pick me up.

Conscious effort will keep your focus on the:

(1) Money you will save,

(2) Speed of implementing,

(3) Certainty of the result.

Moreover, your new confidence is based upon the knowledge that you are using a technique which has been successfully invoked by others. Regardless of what you are told, the NMA is familiar to the executives at your lender's office.

SO, WHAT HAVE YOU GOT TO LOSE?

Getting your due is the next best thing to getting a windfall. The lender will attempt to make you believe that you are not entitled to what you are asking for.

They will act as though it is unheard of to make a loan change in one hour, or even in one week. Everyone else is conditioned to believe that they have to stand in line. The lender tells them whatever excuse is necessary to keep them waiting on their refinance.

Remember, each month you wait for a lowered interest rate is another month of making the higher interest payments on your existing loan.

Your time is their money. Of course, it is out of your pocket.

If you need further convincing to demand your rights, consider this. The lender doesn't let you audit their records or procedures to prove that a bonafide effort has been made to process your loan. You actually don't know what is being done, or not being done by them, to get you your NMA.

In many instances, the lender's attitude is: "How dare you ask if everything has been done to expedite your new loan rate?" In other words, what you don't know won't hurt you.

It might keep your guilt level down to be aware that the lender's willingness to cooperate with the need for your NMA is all you need to get it within a week, a day, or even an hour.

You are only a pawn in their game if you give them absolute control over your financial destiny. If you abdicate, they win. If you persevere, you will win more often than not.

The choice is yours. You will be strung along

as long as you put up with it.
A lot of luck isn't needed.
You need a lot of pluck!

8

The first contact with your lender is making a call to the loan department to get general information. As a consumer, you want to know what is being offered now in comparison to what your present loan is.

If the current rate is at least 2% lower than what you are now paying, the green light should be given to getting the job done as soon as possible.

However, none of us is able to emotionally accept rejection. Some fight on, but 90% give up at the first sign of opposition or obstacles.

It is important to consider the tiers of corporate authority as being a pecking order. Consider that the lower echelon will be least likely to do affirmative action on any procedure outside their customary loan application.

Therefore, you must consider a game plan BEFORE you make your initial contact. Go up, by stages, to each level of authority. If necessary, reach the top rung of the corporate ladder. Use the following order:

(1) Loan service
(2) Loan officer
(3) Loan manager
(4) Branch manager
(5) Executive Vice President
(6) President.

You will not get to speak to the President of many financial institutions. However, you can write "personal and confidential" letters to any individual whose attention you need.

Remember that this is your only loan with Easy Street S&L. They have thousands to be concerned about. But you are not alone. Many others are struggling with similar problems.

There are 87,000,000 owners of real property in the United States. Imagine what would happen if 10% of them demanded NMAs! If only 1% visited their lender's headquarters personally, by phone, or by letter to demand NMAs, think of the impact and the potential for action!

A public relations debacle would be the price of denying simplified changes in terms on existing loans.

You can bet, if the noise got loud enough, more companies would dance to the music. The desires of their constituents, the real estate owners, should be primary.

Could any company absorb the loss of 10,000 customers? Of 100,000? Of 1,000,000?

Each borrower has a bank account someplace. Often it is in the same financial institution, withdrawable at will.

Climb the corporate ladder to the top, if necessary. Then go to your next step, the legal option.

9

Later chapters will tell you how to get quick relief from the high interest rate you are stuck with. Your lender had to anoint you with its good housekeeping stamp of approval for being patient. They patted you on the head, saying: "that didn't taste so bad—did it?"

Now you want to counter the basis used by your lender for mandatory procedures to be followed.

Charges for credit check and report are the most outrageous conceived by the lender.

You have already qualified for your original loan at a time when your property was worth less. Now your equity is greater. That is the real security for the lender.

Obviously the market value of your house or apartment building has significantly increased. Your loan has either remained the same, if you have interest only payments with a balloon payment due at term; OR, has become smaller with principal reductions on each monthly payment.

With a few provisos, you can make an airtight argument for fast reductions in your interest rate and monthly payment. Remember, I didn't say "air-tight" case. There are no guarantees in life. I am only helping you to shift the odds to your favor in successfully rewriting your loan. The chips will be on your side of the table.

First, we take away the "new loan" argument from the lender.

This means you MUST NOT INCREASE your original Trust Deed amount.

This is an indispensible prerequisite to a Note Modification Agreement. The lenders love to increase a $200,000 loan to $210,000, or to whatever sum is necessary to cover your "new loan" costs. This is supposedly doing you a favor. They encourage you to rewrite your loan without taking any money out of your own pocket. They will take it out of your pocket indirectly.

This myth of fallacy enables them not only to charge new loan points on basically the same loan, but allows it to be a "new" loan; thereby allowing the garbage fees to be avoided.

The "favor" to you is when you turn the tables on them!

"I will pay your loan points out of my pocket. I don't want to increase my loan principal balance." Stick to your guns on this position.

The first steps toward winning your battle to get quick relief from oppressive interest rates are:

(1) to show that you are aware of lending procedures, AND,

(2) are willing to facilitate the simplification of the process to obtain the result.

You get them to lower your interest rate to what they are giving the general public. In return, they get a reasonable compensation for their product ($).

If you eliminate the upward change in the principal balance of the existing loan, you are on the way to obtaining not only your objectives, but also eliminating their objections to an NMA.

There are subtleties involved to accomplish your goal of eliminating a new Trust Deed. This paves the way for you to simplify the process of getting your interest rate lowered.

You have now told the loan company that they cannot unilaterally remove their original Deed of Trust from its record priority. This accomplishes 4 things:

(1) Avoids "funding" a new loan through escrow.

(2) Does away with the need for a new appraisal.

(3) Protects the lender by avoiding a new title search and title insurance policy.

(4) Eliminates credit check and report.

When $1.00 of new money is funded, the lender can justify these costly, unnecessary steps. You will see this in greater detail later in this book.

Funding through an escrow, in a traditional refinance, is usually associated with obtaining significantly greater loan funds.

Let's say that, instead of a $200,000 loan being rewritten, that you want $240,000. This is based upon your belief that your property is worth $320,000. This is 75% loan to market value.

Optimumly, you could accomplish this result easier by leaving their first Trust Deed balance intact and by placing a $45,000 Second Trust Deed on the property. This enables you get

$40,000 net new proceeds and pay the costs of both loans.

The negative features of placing a Second Trust Deed are higher interest, higher points and a shorter loan term—generally 1 to 10 years.

Once your decision is made to do business with your existing lender, you take the initiative.

First—you place an innocent sounding call to the Loan Department. You don't disclose your motives upfront. You ask for their quote on terms and costs for the amount you seek as a new borrower.

What you are looking for is evidence that your Bank or S&L is currently in the loan market and what their current terms are. The premises of an NMA is inoperative if your company has withdrawn from the loan marketplace.

If the lender is not now in the lending market, you cannot enforce an NMA even if you have a valid, enforceable Note secured by a Deed of Trust. Neither side to a contract can force the other side to renegotiate unless it is built into the original contract.

After establishing not only the willingness, but eagerness, of your lender to compete in the loan market, the next determinations are the price of the money, the procedures and the time needed to process your transaction. You must always make it clear to the lending agent that you are willing to pay their loan fee. Also be firm in your position that you will not pay for unnecessary procedures and "services."

When they confirm that their current rate is 10%, subject to a new loan application, credit check, appraisal, escrow, and title insurance policy, then you ask to talk to their Loan Modification Department.

Later, we will discuss the reaction of the lender and how you handle yourself.

The request you make, at this point, will be important in speeding the process. Your simple request of an NMA will invariably require you to be shifted to someone with more authority. The loan officer will need to "check it out" and get back to you. Tell them that you expect a return call in 24 hours. Time is money to you. Each payment costs you extra hundreds of dollars per month.

The appraisal is an outmoded procedure, which the loan company justifies, to extract additional profits from you. Assume that the appraiser gets $100 for his time. This is usually one-half of the gross fee if he is an independent contractor. You then see the magnitude of the profit potential in $200 to $500 appraisal fees.

When you seek no new money, you conveniently eliminate their profit, and your expense, in appraising your property which has previously been appraised. The existing loan will be continued in place until you either sell to a new buyer or pay off the loan through refinancing from another lending institution.

There is no way they can remove their Trust Deed from your property unless there is acceleration of a non-assumable loan, by sale or foreclosure.

Understanding the philosophy of why these procedures and costs aren't needed is important for several reasons.

You build strength and confidence in your position. Your conviction of the equity and justice of your contentions is crucial to your ultimate success. Authoritative posture is what they take seriously. Your understanding of "why" the NMA should be done is as important as "how." Otherwise, you never get to the mechanics of making the change.

Steeping yourself in the ideas and reasons for your NMA also gives you moral outrage if you are turned down for a Note Modification.

THE LENDER CANNOT TAKE AWAY YOUR LOAN!

Similarly, you cannot force them to increase your loan amount without satisfying them of your ability to pay and the security of sufficient equity in the property.

An appraisal is only required where new funds are sought. You should not, and must not, give in to this fee or procedure when getting an NMA. It is only a profit generating device.

Credit checks and new financial information are superfluous to prove you are entitled to a lower interest rate and monthly payments.

EXAMPLE "A": "A" gets a $100,000 loan on the purchase of a single family residence in 1981. The loan payment is $1,370 monthly, for principal and interest, with interest at 16% per annum. Rates come down in 1984 to 13%. "A" realizes that he can save approximately $3,000 yearly with a 3% interest rate reduction. The lender tells him: "You don't qualify for a new loan. See us later when you make more money."

Client "A" walks off unhappily. He doesn't

contest the loan rejection. The lender's refusal was unjustified. The irony and the outrageousness of this situation is obvious. "A" can afford to pay $1,370 monthly, but can't afford to pay $1,120 per month!!!

This illustrates the specious and arbitrary denials of relief from high interest rates.

Why is it done? To generate higher return from loans. The higher interest rates on your original loan seem more desirable to the lender than a one time loan fee generated by a refinance.

A lender should not have the right to reapprove existing borrowers who seek only a lowered interest rate and monthly payment. It is outrageous to use the excuse that a customer does not qualifiy for a 10% loan when he is currently paying 13-16% on previously approved credit.

Nobody is forcing you to do business with your existing lender. However, once you do, they should treat you fairly.

Credit reports and checks or financial applications are only for new customers or for "new money."

It is insulting and illogical that you must

prove yourself again. You have already been approved by committee for the original loan. The payments made and kept current by you ratify your credit worthiness.

Reject any additional attempts to require you to again prove your ability to pay.

Escrow fees, in-house or through an independent escrow company, are not required in an NMA.

The new contractual relationship, lowering interest rate and monthly payment, eases your financial burden. It increases protection and enhances security for your lender. You are far less likely to become a problem loan.

Title policies are the fail-safe for escrow, lenders, and borrowers. They are insurance that you get no lien nor encumbrance surprises when you buy real estate. It is false economy to skip escrow or title policy protection in buying real property. Many people have been badly burned by liens on record not known nor disclosed by sellers.

Many "cash back to buyer" deals have defrauded sellers. Lenders in first position have foreclosed on inflated First Trust Deeds. Late recording of owner/seller carried back Seconds have made seller's paper uncollectable. Loan companies have been deprived of knowledge of excessive secondary financing.

There is no change in position in the lender's Deed of Trust under an NMA.

This alleviates the need to insure against intervening liens or encumbrances which jeopardize the seniority of the Lenders's Deed of Trust.

If the original $200,000 First Trust Deed was placed in 1978, then what occurs by an NMA in 1986?

Absolutely nothing! Only the note is modified. The 1978 Trust Deed remains on record, unchanged.

WHAT IS DONE IN COMPUTING THE MONTHLY PAYMENT ON THE MODIFIED LOAN?

The beauty of an NMA is that there is no new loan. A new payment schedule is re-amortized on the years remaining on the original loan. The payments are based on the loan being fully paid in the 22 year balance of your original loan term, not on a new 30 year loan.

Although monthly payments on a 22 year schedule are much higher than 30 year amortization, it is a small price to pay. Your objective is gained by "refinancing" without the so-called garbage fees, which can average $1,500 per $100,000 loan.

The key to your NMA, avoiding the new loan status, is to keep your original Trust Deed on record without recording another instrument. Your NMA gets attached, as an addendum or amendment, to your original note. As such, it doesn't get recorded.

HOW DO YOU GET THE PARITY IN BAR-GAINING POSITION THAT YOU NEED?

You assert your desires as though they are legitimate and grantable by the loan company.

FIRST—you get not only the leverage, but the upper hand. The boldness and audacity of demanding the NMA puts you in an informed and authoritative position with the lender. You show that you have inside information.

SECOND—the alternative to the cooperation of the lender must be the muscle of your options. Your response to non-compliance has to be a threat of legal action. Only a potential lawsuit can alter the odds by tipping the scales in your direction. The scales of justice!

How, and when, you time your action will be

discussed in Chapter 10.

THIRD—you must make it understood, at the start, that you are ready, willing, and able to do business NOW!!!

Your money is immediately available to write a $4,000 check for 2 points on your modified $200,000 loan.

A 2% interest decrease, by itself, will recoup your loan costs in one year!

As a bonus, you can repeat the process again if, and when interest rates go down another few percentage points.

If you intend to keep your property more than a few more years, you are far ahead financially. If the original loan is assumable, and if you sell earlier, the property is more valuable to a buyer. A lowered interest rate increases your cash flow and the property's salability.

You will make inroads in getting relief by letting the lender know that your decision to modify your loan is not debatable, not negotiable, and not exchangeable.

WHY SHOULD YOU ROCK THE BOAT?

Because the risk is small, the cause is just, and you are being reasonable in your willingness to pay for what you get.

Let your handling of the request be dynamic enough to require their response.

Forcing the issue will depend upon the lender's willingness to absorb a public black eye.

Confidentiality of the settlement, and the quietness of an easy and expedient NMA, makes you more powerful in getting your way with lenders.

Consider this. The lender can generate 1000 new loans, with extra fees, WITHOUT LOAN-ING ANY NEW MONEY!

Do you believe they will jeopardize this windfall by fighting publicly with one sour apple who can expose their system? They don't want to educate the public to a secret procedure.

WHAT DO THE LOAN COMPANIES GAIN BY AN NMA?

It is assumed by the lenders that they will lose much revenue by doing NMAs. They eventually may MAKE many millions by advertising available NMAs!

They can advertise: "Come and get it—the 1 hour loans. We refinance INSTANTLY." They will free personnel now tied up in looking over reams of paperwork on unnecessary loan applications.

Freeing employees to process new loans for new borrowers will cut loan processing time. It will shorten from four months to 30-45 days, as in years past. Cheaper, almost non-existent overhead, and good public relations, in becoming the first lender to publicly push NMAs, will be the result.

Now the loan companies are getting tarnished. The image of bankers as respected pillars of society, in three piece suits, is rapidly changing. They are now pillored by society as greedy, distant, and unresponsive to consumer interests.

EXAMPLE "B": Client has a $150,000 loan. His Savings and Loan quotes a 9¾% interest rate, replacing a variable interest loan now at 12%. An oral loan commitment of 30 days is given. The lender "loses the file." Client's credit application is not approved. The loan officer leaves the company. The loan is still not approved for SEVEN MONTHS!

Oral loan commitments aren't worth the paper they aren't written on!

Loan commitments for 30 to 60 days are

worthless where loan processing takes 3 to 4 months, or more. The lender knows upfront, when accepting loan applications, that they can't perform within 60 days. They mislead by continuing to give their word.

Credit is not a factor, but is an excuse, in denying interest rate relief.

This computer age makes current loan processing techniques obsolete. No direct inquiry with loan processing personnel is allowed borrowers, until after the final rejection.

There is a concerted effort, by certain loan companies, to drag their feet. They collect extra interest on the original higher interest rate, until they have milked you to the limit of your patience and endurance.

You must counter this foot dragging by setting YOUR OWN LIMIT. Give them one month for the satisfactory consummation of the easy transaction, executing an NMA.

HOW IS YOUR MUSCLE FLEXED?

You force the lender's hand by writing a letter to the President or CEO (Chief Executive Officer) of the company. Send copies to the loan officer and each person with whom you have had frustrating and inconclusive dealings.

WHAT ARE THE CONTENTS OF THIS DEMAND LETTER?

Typical letters are in Chapter 11 for your adaption to use. The basic points to cover are the specifics of your priorities:

1. A time limit of 10-14 days to consent to an NMA and 30 days for performance by execution of the NMA.

2. Insistance on a 10% fixed interest rate, or whatever is being offered at that time.

3. Time for performance is unconditional.

4. Willingness to tender your points immediately upon lender's acceptance.

5. Demand the NMA form.

6. **Agree to keep the original Trust Deed intact.**

7. Allow the lender to grant your request voluntarily.

8. Reject additional fees. Appraisal, credit reports, escrow or title insurance are all unnecessary.

9. The alternative is a lawsuit. State your theories or Causes of Action.

10. List damages which accrue to you if denied the remedy of an NMA. It is important to

list the difference in the monthly payment between the old rate and the new monthly rate. For example, the 4% difference x $200,000 = $8,000 annually x 22 years remaining = $176,000.

11. Let the lender choose between an NMA and a lawsuit. You would sue for your loss of interest, profits, costs, fees, general and punitive damages.

Let your basic theme be the cooperation between the lender and the consumer. Remind them to keep their word given when they first signed you up. "Of course, when interest rates go down, you will be able to get lower rates." No impediments nor conditions were told you at the time of the original financing.

Now you understand some of the concepts governing the interplay between lender and borrower. Without the basic issues being mastered, you will not master the overall situation. You will have greater difficulty in obtaining lowered interest rate and monthly payment.

Dramatic savings are available on various interest rates and monthly payments between 12-14% and 10%. The contrast is staggering! Remember that your interest amount declines as the principal balance declines. For simplification of figuring your savings on interest, on a constant balance, use simple interest. 1% of $200,000 is $2,000 per year.

So much litigation occurs because of:

(1) Nondisclosure when you start the loan process.

(2) Unwillingness of financial institutions to furnish Notes and Deeds of Trust before funding.

(3) Inadequate training of personnel to thoroughly explain questions to prospective borrowers.

(4) Inattention to details by borrowers. This is partly due to inexperience. Questions are not asked about prepayment penalties, non-assumability, VIR formulas, negative amortization and other conditions buried in small print.

Long ago, we accepted unilateral contracts prepared for, by, and through the lender, as being unalterable and unchallengeable. Until recently, lenders have called the shots in unilateral and arbitrary terms.

Long overdue reforms require either legislative initiative or legal action to do what is equitable. There must be a just balance of interests between the consumer's right to fair treatment, fair documents, and fair charges versus the lender's right to adequate compensation, adequate profit, and adequate security on each transaction.

It is easy to say that the lender has a right to establish his loan requirements and you must either accept them or go elsewhere. You have all heard, or experienced, horror stories of excessive loan charges, at a time when economic expectancies were for lower charges.

EXAMPLE "C" is a last minute disclosure by a loan company.

Loan Company X lends $1,000,000 on an apartment complex purchased by Client "C". "C" learns at COE, when signing loan documents, that there is a 12 month prepayment penalty on the loan payoff. The deal was tied together on a three way property exchange. Both buyer and client expected to pay a 6 month pre-payment penalty, which is the standard in the loan industry.

DO YOU BELIEVE HE ACCEPTED THE LOAN?

Economic duress dictated that he complete the transaction to avoid lawsuits from other parties in the exchange.

Lack of viable choices forced a last minute signature by the borrower. The difference between a 6 month and 12 month prepayment penalty was $12,500!!!

WAS THERE AN ALTERNATIVE FOR CLIENT "C"?

The attitude of the establishment was:

"If you didn't like the loan terms, you should have shopped elsewhere."

HOW COULD THE CLIENT SHOP OTHER PLACES ON THE DAY BEFORE THE CLOSE OF ESCROW?

The answer by the lender, after the fact, was easy. "No" was the answer from the trained seals at the Savings and Loan. "No" is an easy answer by bureaucrats who don't want to jeopardize their job. "No" is said by those who have no authority to adjust the loan.

A common tactic by lenders is to use the exigencies of time to arm twist borrowers. They inject new terms, without prior disclosure, at the last minute.

A lawsuit forced the lender to rebate the surprise excess to client "C".

WHY SHOULD A LAWSUIT BE

NECESSARY?

Why would a settlement be refused? Common fairness dictates an adjustment. The bottom line is that high stakes makes corporate policy. They don't want to disclose their dealings to consumers in either volume or identity.

The method of doing business is part of the problem.

Inadequate advice, inadequate investigation, inadequate time to check documents are all indictable as culprits in misdeeds perpetuated on borrowers.

WHAT CAN BE DONE TO CHANGE PROCEDURES?

Chapter 15 gives some suggestions.

10

Timing is crucial to your being taken seriously by your Savings and Loan. If you delay too long between your initial inquiry and your letter demanding an NMA, you are weakening your case.

Be assertive, be relentless, and be consistent. Be single-minded in your pursuit of the goal stated to the lender. GET YOUR NMA!!!

WHEN DO YOU START?

Each month is time and money lost. Hundreds of excess dollars are being paid, above market interest rates, on your existing loan. Make time work for you, not against you.

1. Read the chapter on letters before writing

your own (Chapter 11). This gives an overview of how tough you need to be in handling of your position and spacing demands.

2. Before writing your first letter, make at least two calls. Call the loan manager and the branch manager, in that order.

DO THIS NOW!

This gives names to quote in your letter to the top officers of the company. Send copies of all follow-up correspondence to these first contacts. This keeps the heat on as many people as possible. The lender's pressure builds up internally for a solution to your problem.

3. Write your firm, but gentle first letter. Show your willingness to do an NMA and your generous offer to pay their loan fee. Give them a big return on a short procedure, the NMA.

4. If you get no response to letter number 1 after 5 days, send demand letter number 2. This demands:

(a) their stated willingness/agreement within 10 days, and

(b) action in 30 days (or before your next payment is due).

5. After the 10 days, send letter #3, if needed. Tell them that they have had ample opportun-

ity to do what is right. Therefore, you will file a lawsuit within 2 weeks. THEN DO IT!

This entire process takes only one month. It gives you a focal point to follow, without agonizing, "should I or shouldn't I?" Do it by the numbers. Do it your way, with language that sounds like you. Use the form letters, entirely or in part, to accomplish your purpose, the obtaining of an NMA.

I have had clients delay action for 2 or 3 years before demanding an NMA. DON'T LET THIS HAPPEN TO YOU!

It's easy to get bogged down in everyday life. Time is money. Money is time. High financial stakes dictate quick action by you, requiring quick response from your lender.

When you make your first request, you must take the stance that it is what you are entitled to. If you act like you are saying "please," it sounds weak, like begging.

If you demand and give ultimatums, you are then forcing the recipient of your missive to consider the risks of non-compliance. The downside risk is to be considered by the executive on the other end. Many times they will acquiesce to a dissident, to shut him/her up by acceding and make money at the same time.

Beware of the price of winning the day. Many times, the granting of the uncommon NMA will be accompanied by a release of all liability. The original loan representations by lender's agents, a confidentiality clause, or other contractual provisions may be up for reconsideration.

My suggestion is to give in on confidentiality where the terms are favorable. Always try to obtain at least one-time assumability and waiver of any prepayment penalties in the original Note as part of the new bargain. Strike while the iron is hot, while they are trying to get rid of a pesky situation. Be firm but pleasant.

HOW HIGH MUST THE FIRES OF DISCONTENT BE RAISED TO GET YOUR RESULT?

You must give a short deadline, a high price to pay if refused, and a promise of further action. A lawsuit.

You must always act as if the burden is on your adversary to take his foot out of the fire. Your lender is your opponent, not your friend. The ball is in their court. If they won't cooperate, that is their problem.

Take the posture that you are supremely and serenely confident of the final results AND that you will win your NMA without appraisal, credit report, escrow, title insurance, or recording expenses because YOU WILL NOT PERMIT THEM.

If they are foolish enough to contest your modest and reasonable demand, then you will be forced to charge your lender attorney's fees and court costs. Remember, you are getting no more than what you are entitled to by Easy Street's promises made at the outset of your business relationship. Your next step is to throw the book at them—THIS BOOK!

Blame your predicament on them.

Blame your instigation on me.

Ask if their loan policies are designed to protect their customers, to protect themselves, or merely to hold onto money until a greasy wheel squeaks. Whenever one's ox is being gored, there is a loud reaction.

You need an equalizer.

This book is your best assurance that you will not go under without a fight. How far you need to go, and how hard you fight, is up to you.

Only YOU can determine whether you can carry this quest out to a conclusion. Decide on a business and on a personal temperament basis.

If the stakes are high enough, you will pursue it.

If you think that possible rewards are matched by depletion of your energies, emotions and time, then you will give up before getting the intended results.

However, you have other options.

You can handle a lawsuit yourself. You can hire a lawyer. You can file a class action which may require waiting 5 years for a conclusion until a full settlement is made for the entire class. You can organize loud, peaceful and non-business interfering demonstrations. You can write letters, or do business elsewhere. You should tell your friends of your sad experience.

The lawsuit will put further pressure on the company. They will then have 30 days under California law to turn it over to their company lawyer, hire outside attorneys, get time for an extension to plead, to file an answer or demurrer (testing the legal sufficiency of the complaint), or to settle.

They will decide whether there will be a fight or flight!

Another decision must be made by the lender. Is the lawsuit a legitimate grievance or is it a "nuisance" case? In other words, is your object a legal holdup for a quick buck, equivalent to blackmail or extortion.

Companies are reluctant to pay out money for past misdeeds. A corporate admission will be hard to rationalize. It also requires adversely amending their bottom line. This is difficult to explain to their shareholders.

Getting prospective advantage gives you more power and persuasion with lenders.

Offer a compromise.

They give you your NMA and you waive attorney's fees, court costs, general and punitive damages. They must do it fast. They must do it without causing you loss of additional sleep, added aggravation, or added expense.

Understand that banks will give away the future to get rid of a present lawsuit. Considering THEIR needs will get you better concessions. Ignoring their practical problems will not only decrease your settlement prospects but also encourage a lengthy, pitched battle.

11

The 3 demand letters cover a 30 day period for requested performance by your lender. What you are looking for is the lender's consent which gives you the opening to write the following:

"As per our conversation of _____, I am confirming our Note Modification Agreement to be prepared by EASY STREET S&L for the loan changes of (1) interest change from 13% to 10% effective upon your receipt of the enclosed loan fee (2) reduction of monthly payment from $2,214 to $1,614."

"All other loan terms are to remain the same. Enclosed is my check for $4,000 which represents a 2% loan fee and payment in full."

LETTER #1

Dear Easy Street:

I have a loan with your company which originated at 13% interest on an original principal balance of $200,000 with monthly payments of $2,214.57. The current balance is $195,000 on loan number RU 1234. It is a single family residence at 888 Rough Road, Los Angeles, CA.

It is my understanding that you are advertising an interest rate of 10%. I accept your offer to the general public for a Note Modification Agreement on my existing loan.

I am not seeking any new funds, nor any extension of my 25 year loan term remaining. I will pay your 2% loan fee of $4,000 out of my own pocket. No new funding is necessary.

Please send me your Note Modification Agreement within 5 days of your receipt of this letter. It is important that the change occur before my next scheduled payment on the first of the month.

Thank you for your anticipated cooperation in this matter.

Sincerely,

I.M. VICTIM

LETTER #2

Dear Easy Street:

I have been informed by your loan department that they are not able to do a Note Modification Agreement on the above loan. No explanation was given except that: "we don't refinance without checking out your loan credit, loan market value, credit and going through a loan escrow."

Please be advised that I am aware that you have a Note Modification Department and can quickly accommodate a change in loan terms.

I am willing to pay the loan fee of 2 points on my existing $200,000 loan. I am NOT willing to pay for a credit report, as I have paid your existing loan for 5 years. Isn't this proof of my good credit? You are my best reference.

No new appraisal, escrow, nor title insurance are necessary, since your original Deed of Trust is remaining on record.

I need your agreement by November 15, 1986 that you will execute a Note Modification Agreement by December 1, 1986. Otherwise, I will be paying $600 extra monthly interest on my loan.

I will withold any further action, pending an amicable resolution of this matter through your Modification Department.

Sincerely,

I.M. VICTIM

LETTER #3

Dear Easy Street:

You are hereby placed on notice that your failure to execute a Note Modification Agreement by December 1, 1986, reducing my 13% interest rate to 10% and my $2,214 monthly payment to $1,614, will be followed by a lawsuit for damages and equitable relief.

I have been frustrated by the run around given by your loan service, loan officers, managers and Note Modification Department. Your denial of a loan change is incomprehensible since you are giving it to strangers.

I am ready, willing, and able to pay your $4,000 loan fee NOW. I am NOT willing to pay escrow, title, appraisal and credit fees. These are unnecessary "services." You know that you can modify my loan in 1 hour rather than 4 months.

If I don't get an affirmative answer for your cooperation, I will file a Complaint in Los Angeles Superior Court. My special damages will be $7,200 per year on my remaining 25 year term, general and punitive damages.

The lawsuit will be for Bad Faith, Unfair Dealing, Interference with Economic Advantage, Breach of Contract, Negligence, Fraud, and Infliction of Emotional Distress.

When I obtained my original loan I was promised that I "could refinance whenever interest rates came down." You have violated this promise.

I will not pay for any fees beyond your loan points. At no time whatsoever was I advised that I would need to requalify for a loan on the existing balance.

It is absurd to put us in the same category with new loan customers. We have established our credit-worthiness.

Have you decided, as a matter of corporate policy, to delay as long as possible the processing of refinances to milk higher interest? If you have, this would be a violation of your duty of fair dealing to me.

Since you are actively and aggressively pursuing new loan business I cannot understand why you are not redoing my own loan.

My legal action will have you live up to your bargain. Many other customers will be waiting to see how you treat me.

Ignore me at your risk. My Complaint will be filed in Superior Court on December 2, 1986.

Sincerely,

I.M. VICTIM

12

Cute new ways are being concocted to get your business now.

Radio commercials tell stories of people who wake up in "heaven," being told they are in a bank, waiting forever for a loan, with lots of charges.

Television commercials show athletic loan reps running and bounding across offices to speed your loan approval and processing.

Particularly galling are mailers, with their half-truths and material non-disclosures.

EXAMPLE: One lender tells its existing borrowers that it is a member of a "select class" of credit-worthy customers who are being offered a quick refinance to lower interest rates and monthly payments, without red tape. Approval is "almost guaranteed."

What isn't being said are how much "garbage" fees for loan processing, loan origination, escrow and "miscellaneous" fees and charges are given the "lucky" customer. Why don't they say it upfront?

They wouldn't get the pigeons to roost on their doorstep without the carrot. They wouldn't get the business if they told the whole story at the outset.

What should be done with this type of deceptive advertising?

Give them what they want—word of mouth publicity. Only one difference. You tell the WHOLE TRUTH—something they won't do.

This is what they don't want to happen. They want the recipients of their "special offer" to keep it hushed up. They want to isolate each borrower, one on one, so they can get their signatures on the contracts, without outside advice.

These same lenders trumpet how fair and fast they are.

You have often heard that "justice delayed is justice denied." A fair loan without speed is ineffective.

The other side of the coin is that speed with unfairness is inequitable. Many erroneous business decisions have been made quickly, without adequate investigations.

It is an abuse of your consumer rights to have the wool pulled over your eyes. How do they think they can get away with this fraud?

Simple. They believe you won't complain or won't know when you have been taken. Don't get in this position. Discuss each "great offer" with someone of greater experience in real estate transactions and loans. Someone of proven reliability, deserving of your trust and confidence should be consulted.

Spread the word to all who will listen to your voice. Tell not only about the people and firms you recommend, but also those to watch closely.

13

Remember the Drivers' Education Course in High School when you learned about your rights in driving a car?

Responsibility was the name of the game. You were taught that a Driver's License is a privilege and not a right.

It is the same way with lenders. They expect you to "know" that it is a privilege when you get the loan. It should feel like an important rite of passage, worthy of celebration. They place it on the same plateau as your wedding, the birth of your first child, landing the big account, getting your first job, and hitting a home run.

All is set for the underdog—YOU—to be allowed to be the winner, for a price. THEIR price.

Why is it so?

It's because we cater to them. Savings and Loans only go after our business when their loan volume is down or their earnings are sagging.

We must drive a harder bargain. Before we can do so, we must have greater clout. The reputation of those lenders who treat their clients fairly is very quickly known in the real estate community. Those who gouge, whenever they have an opportunity, should also be well publicized.

No lending institution is invulnerable to problems. We're going to give them a black eye, unless they play fair. Fair means not to generate greater income only by throwing obstacles in your path to a modified loan.

You now know where the goal line is. The fastest way there is a direct path. Go through the holes in their "lines." You have the chips. The arguments and procedures here are your strong suit. Soon you will have the right, and not just the privilege, to get your Note Modification

Agreement. You will no longer be at the mercy of others. You will set the table. Then you will enjoy the feast that you have worked so hard for.

14

Salesmen know the pivotal moment where the deal is hanging in the balance. It is called the "make or break" point.

There is a delicate psychological point in each transaction where it appears that the results hang by a thread. This may be an illusion built upon fear of failure. There is no scientific basis that any set of circumstances is paramount in influencing the other party to the transaction.

This is not a myth. You must correctly calculate the most telling arguments, for others to glom onto, to justify the NMA.

The lenders have their own fears:

(1) Fear of a lawsuit;

(2) Fear of losing money;

(3) Fear of having a bad loan on the books;

(4) Fear of bad publicity;

(5) Fear of offending good customers;

(6) Fear of losing business;

(7) Fear of looking bad in the eyes of officers or executives;

(8) Fear of losing their jobs in the next office review or audit;

(9) Fear of complaints about their treatment of customers;

And so on.

You thought your fears of being turned down for your "refinance" were out of sight!

Play these corporate fears like a fiddle. The threat to them is worse than you actually playing the cards in your hand.

You have your own fears:

(1) Is a lawsuit costly?

(2) Do the benefits outweigh the risks?

(3) How long will it take?

(4) Is it worth the aggravation?

(5) Can my nerves stand the tension?

(6) Can I stand being in limbo for very long?

(7) Will I look like a fool?

(8) Will they call my loan?

It's a battle of weaknesses!

Make it a battle of your STRENGTHS VS. their WEAKNESSES! Look at the weak points in their armor.

WHERE IS YOUR LENDER VULNERABLE?

If you know they have a Note or Loan Modification Department—play that card.

"ARE YOU DISCRIMINATING AGAINST ME?" This is a biggie in these days of equal treatment.

"Why would you do it for Joe Schmoe and not for me?"

"What difference is it that I have a judgment against me? I'm paying your loan! How can you turn me down when you are giving loans to strangers.

"Do you want me to take my CD across the street? Maybe they will treat me better."

Remember the "temporary" insurance your S&L placed on your property when your fire insurance wasn't renewed within 5 days? They said it was to "protect their interest." They made 500% profit for 2 months, despite your renewal of the annual permanent insurance.

A leading company has a subsidiary "insurance" company which automatically goes into gear if they don't get a renewal policy ONE MONTH before expiration! Nobody renews their fire insurance that early.

The outrage that you can, and must, muster is important to convince the lender of your determination to follow through.

Try it. You'll often like the results.

You either scare a subordinate (loan officer) or convince a Vice President (bank manager) of the desirability of cooperating with you. You have played ball with them for so many years.

This is not a game for the timid.

Change from Peter Parker to Spiderman, or from Clark Kent to Superman. Make the bank inner sanctum your telephone booth.

Stand up and yell out the window: "I'm mad and I'm not going to take it anymore."

You've seen enough movies to know that the winning poker hand isn't seen by the opponent who folds his cards. Play your hand right and you'll win more often than not.

Believe in your cause. Your opponent, the lender, will understand that you are not to be trifled with by a denial of your NMA.

Remember that the lender may hate to make the NMA now, but they will love it in years to come. They will realize the huge potential of the ready-made existing loans market. Your loan may be rolled over, for a fee, several times during the life of the loan.

They will love making thousands of dollars of loan fees in one hour.

Convince them that it is a win-win situation. It is a quick, no risk, modification for them. The NMA stops the endless loan processing wait for you.

Why should they risk the bad-mouthing from their loan customers for being unresponsive.

You will be amazed how this caps the discussion!

If they aren't totally insensitive to their image AND their pocketbook, you will be wearing the broad smile of victory. Then tell your love: "Look, honey—we got the money."

15

You must get used to the idea that there is no substitute for personal time spent in investigating available loans.

It is amazing how buyers of $200,000 properties spend one-tenth the time as with a $20,000 automobile purchase. They must kick the financial tires of their real property investments.

Many times they leave their financial decision to the loan department of the bank handling their savings accounts. Or else they read ads to choose a Mortgage Broker at 1-2 points premium above the loan fees. They have someone else obtain the loan for them, even if they have no credit problem or if conventional loans are readily available.

We must establish, as an industry standard, either on demand or by legislative reform, the right to TDs and Promissory Notes, upon demand. These should be made available to us by each prospective lender at the time we make our initial inquiries. We must know the FULL package being offered to us. This is an indispensable right.

Next, we must have a written disclosure of all loan processing charges before making a loan application.

Finally, we must have available information as to Fixed versus VIR rates, open ended or capped VIR; assumability, prepayment penalties, time for processing the loan, written loan commitments, time for appraisal, credit checks, and escrow fees in full.

If any of the above is denied or refused—say SAYONARA!

Good work and good results require your open inquiry. You should expect to get consumer answers. You are entitled to complete and accurate information. No less can be expected in order to make intelligent choices.

The lending industry has insulted our intelligence long enough by saying: "sign here." Rush acts caused by lenders' secret procedures, indifference and lack of empathy for the individual's plight have amounted to almost a wanton diregard for the consequences to the borrower.

Financing is the underpinning for the consummation of most transactions. Otherwise, resulting chaos haunts many buyers for years.

In the future, we must be assured that chastened lenders will bargain in good faith in negotiating and fully disclosing the loan package.

EXAMPLE "D": A mortgage broker advertises in a respected metropolitan newspaper about his low interest, fixed rate, Trust Deeds with fast funding. Our client calls the mortgage broker.

The client is told that the lender will process this competitive loan at little or no risk to him. There is one catch. Since it is backed by a federal agency's money, the lender requires $1,500 to begin processing the loan.

"O.K.", says the client. "It sounds good. In fact, it sounds so good that I will apply for THREE new loans on your offer. Here is $4,500 to cover upfront fees for a 10 unit, 8 unit, and a 9 unit building. I am so happy that I saw your ad. I can get rid of my crazy existing financing and have certainty of my cash flow for years to come."

Papers are filled out, income tax and financial statements provided, and loan processing begins.

Next, the appraiser comes out to look at the buildings. "Everything is go," says the company. "However, it is required that you do a termite clearance on the 10 units, a paint job on the 3 units, and repair woodwork on the 9 unit building."

$8,000 later—the client is told: "Congratulations, you got the loans. We will fund in two days. Sign these 15 pages of loan terms and conditions."

The client reads the letter agreement. He is wondering why the Mortgage Broker has a clause giving him veto power over the owner's hiring and firing of management for each building. He raises an eyebrow on a paragraph limiting advance rents to one month. The borrower is astounded by the requirement that profit and loss statements and tax returns must be provided annually.

WHAT WOULD THE LENDER DO IF THE FINANCIAL INFORMATION IS NOT FILED? Would the lender, or servicing agent, foreclose on the properties—even if the payments are current?

The client tells the lender, "I had no intention of abdicating control over my holdings to you. I didn't seek a partner, only a loan."

In demanding the return of the $8,000, I was told by the owner of the mortgage company: "Why, we had no other complaints on the $50,000,000 in loans written last year."

I replied: "How many of your borrowers were told about your restrictive conditions at the time they made their application and you took their money? I BET YOU WOULDN'T BE IN BUSINESS IF YOU DISCLOSED YOUR "REQUIREMENTS" FIRST, RATHER THAN AFTER ROPING IN THE BORROWERS."

It took one month to settle the case after the lawsuit was filed.

EXAMPLE "E": The client obtains a 9½% First Trust Deed Loan in 1977 when rates were similar to 1986. The borrower is quoted 10% fixed vs. 9½% variable. He is pushed to take the variable and "save money." Literature handed to the client says there is a possible 2½% rate adjustment over the life of the loan.

Five years later, on the anniversary date of the original loan, the owner gets a letter advising of an interest rate change in 45 or 60 days. Since there were no numbers in the letter, there was no incentive to save it.

Sure enough, the loan company followed through with an increase of the original interest rate—to 15.75%!!!

How does this happen?

Easy. The cost of money under the monthly statistics of the FHLB (Federal Home Loan Bank) Eleventh District in San Francisco was 12.537% in February, 1982. The note provided for 306 "basis points" tacked onto the cost of the money. This set the second five year rate at 15.75%.

WHAT DOES THE CONSUMER DO
FOR RELIEF?

He can't refinance easily when rates are high. There would be an impossible interest rate with a new lender. The owner would also pay loan fees and the familiar new loan charges of appraisal, credit report, escrow, title insurance, recording fees, etc.

He can beef to his lender. "Hey, this is wrong and not what I was quoted. I would have taken the fixed rate loan, rather than the VIR, if I had known I was going to be raked over like this. My apartment building now has a big negative cash flow. The new interest rate, thanks to you, makes the property unsalable. I am being drained financially and emotionally by this unexpected rip-off."

WHAT IS THE LENDER'S RESPONSE?

"Gee, we're sorry:

A. "The 2.5% interest rate cap was only for 1 to 4 units. Unfortunately, you have 5 units;

B. "Your loan officer/mortgage broker wasn't authorized to tell you that;

C. "The agent who told you that doesn't work here any longer; or,

D. "You know, that despite whatever you have been told, the oral representations are superseded by the written contracts you signed. Of course, you thoroughly read the Note, Deed of Trust, Loan Package Agreement—didn't you?"

At this point, the stonewalling is your downfall if your complaint goes no further. The "You can't fight City Hall" concept, intimidates the borrower. The situation doesn't get adjusted if there is no persistence in seeking legal redress.

Only the threat of, or the actual start of litigation will change this scenario. We can correct the abuses so rampant in the real estate loan industry.

EXAMPLE "F": The owner of a large apartment building says to a new lender: "I'm trying to save my 50 unit apartment building. It needs upgrading. I don't have the funds to do it. I'm facing a foreclosure which my Bankruptcy can't stop forever. Can you help me?"

"Why sure, partner. You have come to the right place. We can give you $500,000 to pay off your overdue obligations, based on the property equity rather than on your credit. We know you have a temporary money crunch, but we will help you out. You will only have to pay us 16% interest and 8 points loan fee ($40,000). We will beat your foreclosure sale date."

The delighted owner signs the application and plans to rebuild his shattered business empire.

The foreclosure day or reckoning is Monday at 9:00 A.M. On Friday at 4:00 P.M., our owner appears as scheduled, to sign closing papers and receive his loan funds. He gets the correct amount of his loan ($500,000), and the loan fee of $40,000 is correct. The client is flabbergasted to see listed $5,000 in attorney's fees and $1,000 for loan preparation fee. Neither had been previously disclosed.

You know what my client did. He took the loan under the pressure of losing the property. He loudly protested the undue economic duress.

The lender took advantage of the owner's desperate financial bind. They knew he had no choice but to eat the last minute surprises. The lender didn't anticipate that the client would get mad and later get even. The money was returned. The inequitable abuse was remedied.

How many people don't fight these situations and thus get ripped off by the MO (Modus Operandi) of legalized theft? Too many unscrupulous lenders take advantage of the borrower's needs by injecting last minute, unauthorized charges. THE UNCLEAN HANDS NEED WASHING!

16

After four months of waiting, your escrow calls and says: "Congratulations, your loan is approved! Come down and sign the 15 pages of documents so we can fund on Monday and record on Tuesday."

At 4:59 P.M. on Friday afternoon, the buyer has a few minutes to study a mass of technical and unfamiliar material. He or she has as much chance of communicating with his Real Estate Broker or Lawyer at this time of day as the man in the moon.

WHY HAVE BUILT IN DISAPPOINTMENT AND DISASTER?

Perhaps the rush act is caused by limited

funding time. The lender has to limit the time that their loan money is out of action. They need the "float" to earn interest by fast placement of their cash.

This desire for 48 hour funding is independent of the borrowers's need. The documents must be disclosed in advance of the fateful day of signing.

WHY NOT HAVE PROTOTYPES OF LOAN DOCUMENTS SUPPLIED 30 DAYS BEFORE COE, INSTEAD OF 30 MINUTES IN ADVANCE?

What prevents the Note and Deed of Trust, on assumable loans, from being furnished buyers in escrow by loan companies? Too often, sellers misplace their loan papers or innocently misrepresent them to real estate brokers, escrow and buyers.

So little care and so much damage!!

More time and more caution minimizes damages and lawsuits.

Fuller education and disclosure benefits all of us in these transactions.

Another lender trick, to earn extra money, is to fund late in the week so that their check doesn't clear until Monday. If escrow closes on Friday, this gives three days extra interest on the "float."

This is the equivalent of having an eight day hold on checks cashed by banks or deposited in checking and savings accounts. They clear them in two days and get six days extra interest without any financial investment.

Double interest is double dealing!

We need special legislation to prevent the rush jobs and the lack of comprehension of loan terms caused thereby.

The lenders could voluntarily comply, but won't. They must give the documents earlier.

Perhaps they are afraid of the borrowers having too much time to reconsider the transaction.

We must make the lenders afraid of the consequences if they DON'T give early disclosure of important documents on your deal.

17

I was privileged to meet consumer advocate Ralph Nader, some years ago, when he spoke at a Los Angeles Trial Lawyers meeting I chaired. His phrase—"Crime in the streets has become crime in the suites,"—stuck with me. It dramatically illustrated corporate indifference.

He meant that white collar crime took on new meaning by corner cutting, consumer rip-offs, and just plain neglect. Motivated by greed in draining the last buck of profit from your pocket.

We hear about wonderful support by Banks and S&Ls of their communities. They are "good citizens." They get good PR. But where does charity begin? Where do good deeds end?

The answer is that charity begins at home—your home. The good solid citizen, YOU, should receive your own reward. It isn't a gift. It is what you are entitled to in good faith and fair dealing by your lender.

Don't kid yourself. You aren't the object of your lender's philanthropy.

If you were higher in their consciousness, you would receive ALL the loan documents at the time you applied for the loan. Not as an afterthought at the end.

Is it intended that you be rushed into signing documents in 30 minutes? It sure seems so. Do they think you read 10,000 words per minute? They know you can't read all the fine print. Is there something they are trying to hide by not initially disclosing? Only they know. You have your suspicions later, when you discover the:

(1) prepayment penalty;

(2) non-assumability clause;

(3) the transfer fee;

(4) the variable formula;

(5) negative amortization;

(6) accrued interest;

(7) changes from 30 to 40 year term of loan;

(8) add on fees.

How do they reconcile keeping you in the dark on important conditions?

Why do lenders or loan agents say that your refinance is a snap? They know, all along, they will charge fees beyond the points. Why don't they say upfront, "Look, we have our bottom-line needs to stay in business. You will be subject to our terms at that time. We can't lock your future fees in now. We will be competitive, but we make no guarantees."

That would be an honest statement.

What they really do is different. We are led down the primrose path, flowers strewn ahead of us, with sweet lullabies being crooned about us living happily forever in the home they helped us buy.

Is this reality or is it an illusion?

Make your own realities by insisting on written promises. Don't be lulled into signing your loan package without them. If the representations aren't solid enough to put on paper, they are probably worthless. I've had many cases where the tongue and ear were mightier than the pen and paper.

Don't rely on the swan song or it might be the last sweet music you hear in the lender's symphony of discordant notes.

IS THE GAME NECESSARY?

Why do you think loan companies keep people waiting in line to process their loans? Are their people slow workers?

You are given many forms to establish your identity. They check references, credit, job, real property liens, IRS liens, judgments, bad rumors—you name it.

If you were an ex-con, con man, or the perpetrator of a fraud on a creditor, all this checking would be justified. If you have no judgments beyond "Peoples' Court" in Small Claims, and you paid sufficient down payment AND if they trust their own appraiser—what is their risk to loan primarily upon the equity in your property?

If you should drop a $300,000 home with a $60,000 down payment, the lender gets a large windfall. So often, the windfall is enhanced by inflation to $400,000! This is not a highly leveraged loan which they should fear. They can easily absorb a few months' loss of income.

What does the borrower gain by losing such a large down payment? Can they be so naive to think you wouldn't scrape and scrounge around to keep your biggest investment afloat? Do they really believe you wouldn't move heaven and earth to make your payments on that nice roof over your head?

If you had paid only 5% down on a $100,000 home, they would have cause for alarm. The lender then should play it close to the vest. A 5% commission on a REO resale would instantly wipe out their equity. Each month gives the lender a loss on this non-performing and unwanted asset.

Let's examine the need for speed. Each week in escrow jeopardizes the buyer and seller. Each has additional opportunity to file a Notice of Cancellation.

You say, "The seller or buyer can't cancel if they aren't entitled to." The buyer or seller has the POWER to stop an escrow in its tracks.

When an escrow takes 4 months, due to slow loan processing, it has much more risk of not closing. A 60 day escrow was the industry standard until 1985. The seller may change his mind about selling or there is buyer's remorse. Liquidated damages allows a forfeiture up to 3% of the sales price in California. Where damages are difficult to estimate, the parties may stipulate to a fixed sum as conclusive. What happens if there is no forfeiture clause in the escrow instructions?

This may shock you.

ABSOLUTELY NOTHING HAPPENS!

The escrow, as neutral stakeholder, is powerless to decide which party is intitled to the deposit. The money is frozen until one party sues to kill or force the deal. Then the escrow "interpleads" the money into court to decide who is entitled to it.

Now that you are aware of the chaos made possible by a Notice of Cancellation, you can see how lender-created delays kill deals, profits, broker commissions, escrow costs AND YOUR EXPECTATIONS.

Don't the lenders care about efficiency? Don't they care about image? Can't they invent a better mousetrap? Can't they be more responsive to the needs of the people?

Is this game necessary?

A resounding NO!

We go along because it's the only game in town. We have become used to it. Think about it. If loans took one year, it would devastate the real estate market!!

Perhaps there should be penalty clauses in loan contracts providing that if either party delays, negligently or intentionally, the timely closing of an escrow, per diem penalties would be charged.

Incentives to perform are needed. If they don't work, get new incentives or new lenders.

Consider the alternative. Go about "business as usual" and continue to kill hundreds of millions in escrow which never close.

Look at escrow officers.

Notice the high percentage who chain-smoke, have nervous disorders, long hours, or miss lunches. They have constant deadlines. They must continually court new business in order to stay in business. It's one tough job. I would not want it for any amount of money. Lenders' procrastinations make escrow officers' days a little longer and a lot harder.

Lenders, are you listening? Isn't there a better way OR are your delays a cover for incompetence or greed? You indict or clear yourself by service. Is it to be service to yourself or to the public you profess to serve.

Do your job right. The public will beat a path to your door.

Do your job wrong. The public will beat a path to the Court House.

The choice is yours.

18

Real wealth in the United States has been buttressed by real estate investments. Robert E. Lee, the famous Confederate Civil War General, bought land and never sold. Escrow officers would have hated him.

Will Rogers once said, "Buy land. They ain't making any more of it."

Many fortunes have been made on modest beginnings. Even Bank of America bailed itself out of red ink by selling for $58,000,000 a property purchased for $50,000 thirty years earlier!!!!

There is a fine line between a lender making

over-leveraged loans and having the courage of its convictions in making faster loan decisions.

Few deals are 100% cash from the buyer. The U.S. economy has its underpinning on quick, accessible loans, to fuel a healthy economy.

How long can a stagnant economy suffer the indifference of Banks and S&Ls?

How long can lenders continue their stage-coach speed? They are failing at a greater rate in the 1980s than in any period since the Great Depression.

The tortoise beat the hare. The bankers' crawl is not a new dance. It is ridiculous.

The race is to the swift. The lender who continues to delay will earn its epitaph.

Roulette is spinning the wheel of fortune to get, hopefully, a winning number. Real estate transactions command certainty, not random chance. Buying and selling property is a high stakes game. It deserves better.

Refinancing is also part of the American Dream.

Are there any of us who obtained a 13-18% loan in 1981-83 who didn't expect to refinance when rates got down to 10%? Kicking dirt in our faces kills the dream suddenly and unexpectedly.

Have the guts to demand of lenders, at the beginning: "I want to be guaranteed in writing, NOW, the required loan fees, processing time and procedures when I modify my loan later. Otherwise we can't do business. Disclose now, or close out my application now. I won't waste your time, don't waste mine!"

HOW DO REAL ESTATE BROKERS ASSIST YOU IN GETTING YOUR NMA?

It would be nice to believe that brokers will fight for your rights. Some conscientious agents will take up your battles, as their own, independent of their pocketbook.

But face it. At the time you need an NMA, the broker has already made his commission. Brokers will learn that NMAs make a healthier real estate market, and protect commissions by closing a higher percentage of deals opened.

Brokers in the know are almost unanimous in supporting the right to an NMA. They also can decide, more than any other group, which financial institutions deserve to get our business. Think of the potential to positively influence corporate lending and responsibility!

REACH FOR YOUR GOAL!

Don't take "no" for an answer any more than your lender should take your business for granted. Follow the guidelines and arguments in this book. You have the makings of success in the making of your NMA.

19

Every lawyer should have a gut feeling when conduct by an adversary, or potential adverse party, is outrageous conduct which shocks the sensitivities or conscience of TARM (The Average Reasonable Man).

Unfortunately, TARM doesn't have much feel for this condition, except to believe he or she has been "taken" and that there must be something that can be done about it.

Your legal weapon is the lawsuit. Your remedy is punitive damages.

Punitive damages, based upon intentional breach of contract, fraud, bad faith, unfair dealing, or other intentional or malicious wrongdoing is compensable.

The size of the damages to punish the wrong-doer and reward the innocent party may be speculative.

You can hone your instincts for what is outrageous. You know that waiting three to five years for a jury to ratify your case is frustrating. What you need is an advance barometer which is reliable within a small margin of error.

What is this gauge?

PEOPLE! PEOPLE! PEOPLE!

Run your story by your own jury first, one at a time. Tell them your sad tale. Don't put words in their mouths. Ask them what their first reaction is to what happened to you. Don't argue your case with them. Give facts concisely, without embellishment.

Chances are, you will hear words like "ridiculous," "crooked," "wrong," or "shouldn't have happened," as well as "outrageous."

Don't ask only your close friends and relatives. They would naturally be supportive. You don't want a biased point of view to influence your plan of attack.

After you get your cross-section of public

opinion, you will be more confident that pursuit of your NMA through legal avenues is justified. You will believe in the probability of success when you get to a trial on the merits of your case.

Most likely you won't have to try your case, even though you may have to file it in court.

The lender, if wise, would be best advised to settle quietly and cheaply by giving you what you need and want, so long as it is reasonable.

20

This Chapter has two sample Complaints (Lawsuits) which have been prepared for use in California. They are to be used after your rope has been extended to its limit by rejection of your demand letters.

The theories upon which you are suing are entitled "Causes of Action." They are also known as "Counts." You should consult an attorney to review any legal pleading, adapted to your use, before filing it with the Superior Court.

Complaint #1 is the "long form." It may be fleshed out by relating your individual facts in much greater detail.

The Defendants who are served with a copy of the Complaint have several options. They may file an Answer within 30 days contesting your action. It can be a general denial of your claims with Affirmative Defenses. Defenses may include "failure to state facts sufficient to constitute a Cause of Action" or "lack of Consideration."

Another possible response is a "Demurrer." This is a pleading which tests the sufficiency of another pleading. It says, in effect: "so what?" The Demurrer may be on technical grounds, such as Uncertainty. This is a "Special Demurrer" and may be easily remedied by an Amended Complaint. A "General Demurrer" may attack your entire action by raising the Statute of Frauds (requiring certain real estate promises to be in writing) or the the Statute of Limitations (that your action is "stale" or beyond the time limit).

Stating a Cause of Action adequately to get by a Demurrer is different than proving your case at the time of trial. High priced defense lawyers may put your attorney through the wringer to state your theories as required under applicable pleading rules.

Your Complaint is the first pleading in the case. It does two things:

1. It shows you mean business. Your threats have been followed up with the action promised.

2. It puts the ball in their court, as well as in Court. Pressure is placed on the Defendants to file a responsive pleading, get an extension of time from you or your attorney, or talk settlement with you.

You can be sure that your claim will be read and your Complaint responded to, formally or informally.

The Complaint starts the court proceedings. A settlement or verdict ends the case.

Read each Sample Complaint at least twice. First read it casually, for feel, without pressuring yourself to grasp every phrase. Next, read the commentary on each Complaint, before reviewing, to cement your understanding of the forms and procedure.

SUMMONS
(CITACION JUDICIAL)

NOTICE TO DEFENDANT: *(Aviso a Acusado)*
EASY STREET SAVINGS AND LOAN ASSOCIATION, a
California Corporation; DOES 1 to 200, inclu-
sive; DOE CORPORATIONS 1 to 200, inclusive;
DOE PARTNERSHIPS 1 to 200, inclusive.

YOU ARE BEING SUED BY PLAINTIFF:
(A Ud. le está demandando)
I.M. VICTIM and MAY BEE VICTIM.

You have *30 CALENDAR DAYS* after this summons is served on you to file a typewritten response at this court.	*Después de que le entreguen esta citación judicial usted tiene un plazo de 30 DIAS CALENDARIOS para presentar una respuesta escrita a máquina en esta corte.*
A letter or phone call will not protect you; your typewritten response must be in proper legal form if you want the court to hear your case.	*Una carta o una llamada telefónica no le ofrecerá protección; su respuesta escrita a máquina tiene que cumplir con las formalidades legales apropiadas si usted quiere que la corte escuche su caso.*
If you do not file your response on time, you may lose the case, and your wages, money and property may be taken without further warning from the court.	*Si usted no presenta su respuesta a tiempo, puede perder el caso, y le pueden quitar su salario, su dinero y otras cosas de su propiedad sin aviso adicional por parte de la corte.*
There are other legal requirements. You may want to call an attorney right away. If you do not know an attorney, you may call an attorney referral service or a legal aid office (listed in the phone book).	*Existen otros requisitos legales. Puede que usted quiera llamar a un abogado inmediatamente. Si no conoce a un abogado, puede llamar a un servicio de referencia de abogados o a una oficina de ayuda legal (vea el directorio telefónico).*

CASE NUMBER: *(Número del Caso)*

The name and address of the court is: *(El nombre y dirección de la corte es)*
SUPERIOR COURT OF THE STATE OF CALIFORNIA
FOR THE COUNTY OF LOS ANGELES
111 North Hill Street
Los Angeles, California
CENTRAL DISTRICT

The name, address, and telephone number of plaintiff's attorney, or plaintiff without an attorney, is:
(El nombre, la dirección y el número de teléfono del abogado del demandante, o del demandante que no tiene abogado, es)
MICHAEL D. HILLER, Esq.
16055 Ventura Boulevard
Suite 603
Encino, CA 91436
Telephone: (818) 990-7843

DATE: Frank S. Zolin,   Clerk, by _____, Deputy
(Fecha)   *(Actuario)*   *(Delegado)*

[SEAL]

NOTICE TO THE PERSON SERVED: You are served
1. ☐ as an individual defendant.
2. ☐ as the person sued under the fictitious name of *(specify)*:

3. ☐ on behalf of *(specify)*:

   under: ☐ CCP 416.10 (corporation)   ☐ CCP 416.60 (minor)
          ☐ CCP 416.20 (defunct corporation)   ☐ CCP 416.70 (conservatee)
          ☐ CCP 416.40 (association or partnership) ☐ CCP 416.90 (individual)
          ☐ other:
4. ☐ by personal delivery on *(date)*:

Form Adopted by Rule 982
Judicial Council of California
982(a)(9) [Rev. January 1, 1984]

(See reverse for Proof of Service)
SUMMONS

76S818B - 9-85

CCP 412.20

1 MICHAEL D. HILLER
  16055 Ventura Boulevard
2 Suite 603
  Encino, CA 91436
3 Telephone: (818) 990-7843

4 Attorney for Plaintiffs

5

6

7

8   SUPERIOR COURT OF THE STATE OF CALIFORNIA

9   FOR THE COUNTY OF LOS ANGELES

10

11 I.M. VICTIM and MAY BEE   )   CASE NO.
   VICTIM,   )
12   )   COMPLAINT FOR:
             Plaintiffs,   )
13   )   1. TEMPORARY RESTRAINING ORDER AND
   vs.   )   PERMANENT INJUNCTIONS
14   )   2. DECLARATORY RELIEF
   EASY STREET SAVINGS AND   )   3. INTERFERENCE WITH ECONOMIC ADVAN-
15 LOAN ASSOCIATION, a Cali-)   TAGE
   fornia Corporation; DOES   )   4. EQUITABLE ESTOPPEL
16 1 to 200, inclusive; DOE   )   5. CONSTRUCTIVE TRUST
   CORPORATIONS 1 to 200,   )   6. QUIET TITLE
17 inclusive; DOE PARTNER-   )   7. BREACH OF FIDUCIARY DUTY
   SHIPS 1 to 200, inclu-   )   8. PROMISSORY ESTOPPEL
18 sive,   )   9. BAD FAITH
)   10. BREACH OF WARRANTY
19   )   11. BREACH OF CONTRACT
             Defendants.   )   12. FRAUD
20 _____)   13. NEGLIGENCE
                                  14. INFLICTION OF EMOTIONAL DISTRESS
21   //   //   15. CONFLICT OF INTEREST
                                  16. FAILURE OF FAIR DEALING
22   17. ACCOUNTING
                                  18. UNJUST ENRICHMENT
23   //   19. REFORMATION

24 PLAINTIFFS ALLEGE:

25   FIRST CAUSE OF ACTION

26   TEMPORARY RESTRAINING ORDER AND PERMANENT INJUNCTIONS

27   1. At all times herein mentioned the Plaintiffs and Defen-

28 dants were residents of the County of Los Angeles, State of Cali-

1 fornia.

2   2. (a) At all times mentioned herein, Defendants EASY
3 STREET SAVINGS AND LOAN and DOE CORPORATIONS 1 to 200, inclusive,
4 were California corpoations, organized and existing under the laws
5 of the State of California.

6   (b) DOE PARTNERSHIPS 1 to 200, inclusive, are Partner-
7 ships, organized and existing under the laws of the State of Cali-
8 fornia.

9   3. The true names and capacities, whether individual, cor-
10 porate, associate, or otherwise of Defendants named herein as DOES
11 1 to 200, inclusive; DOE CORPORATIONS 1 to 200, inclusive; DOE
12 PARTNERSHIPS 1 to 200, inclusive, are unknown to Plaintiffs, who
13 therefore sue said Defendants by such fictitious names and Plain-
14 tiffs will ask leave to amend this Complaint to show their true
15 names and capacities when the same has been ascertained.

16   4. At all times herein mentioned, the Defendants, and each
17 of them, were the agents, employees and employers of each of their
18 co-defendants and in doing the things hereinafter alleged, were
19 acting within the course and scope of said agency and employment
20 with consent and knowledge of each other.

21   5. On October 23, 1981, Plaintiffs became the legal owners
22 of the real property legally described as Lot 1 of Tract 2, as per
23 Map recorded in book 3, page 4, parcel 5, commonly described as
24 888 Rough Road, Los Angeles, County of Los Angeles, State of Cali-
25 fornia.

26   6. Defendant EASY STREET SAVINGS AND LOAN ASSOCIAITON, de-
27 fendants, and each of them, loaned $200,000.00 to Plaintiffs on a
28 30 year fully amortized fixed-rate loan, payable $2214.28 per

month at 13% per annum, secured by a Note and Deed of Trust on subject real property supra.

Plaintiffs obtained said loan on the express representations
by Defendants, and each of them, that the loan could be refinanced
at any time thereafter, for a one-time loan fee of 2% of the
principal balance, whenever the interest rates became lower than
13% per annum, the initial rate under loan number RU 1234.

Plaintiffs became Trustors and EASY STREET, the beneficiary
of subject real property loan on a fixed rate of 13% on the refinance representation of 2% loan fee, with no additional charges or
costs.

7. On October 23, 1986, Plaintiffs approached EASY STREET
to refinance said loan, when said loan had a principal balance of
approximately $195,000.00 and market loan rates for single family
residences, such as Plaintiffs' was at or under 10% per annum,
for 30 year fixed-rate loans. At said time, Defendants, and each
of them quoted 10% per annum fixed rate loan with 2% loan fee plus
$350.00 appraisal fee, $100 credit check charges, $400 escrow fees,
and various other charges which were unnecessary and unwarranted
for said refinance.

Plaintiffs learned that a 10% per annum interest rate would
result in a monthly savings of approximately $600. Despite a low-
er payment by a refinance at lower interest rates, Defendants, and
each of them, demanded a credit report and application to be prepared and paid for by Plaintiffs and a reappraisal of subject real
property, to be paid for by Plaintiffs.

Alternatively, Plaintiffs sought an increase in the loan
amount to approximately $240,000.00 which at 10% interest per an-

num, would have resulted in monthly payments of principal and interest of $2214.28 or below Plaintiffs' existing monthly payment
paid by Plaintiffs for the past 5 years.

Defendants, and each of them, approved Plaintiffs' credit for
a $2214.28 monthly payment in October, 1981 when subject property
was appraised and purchased by Plaintiffs for $320,000.

Defendants, and each of them, have a loan policy of lending
up to 75% of market value and knew that the loan value of subject
residence was $240,000.00 and that inflation since October 24,
1981 guaranteed a market value of subject real property of
$320,000.00 or more in October, 1986.

8. Defendants' attempts to enforce refinance loan fees of 2%
plus appraisal, credit, escrow, title policy, and other various
fees and charges, with or without additional loan proceeds places
an unnecessary and unwarranted financial burden and economic duress
on Plaintiffs, contrary to the contractual agreements and assurances Plantiffs received when obtaining said loan from EASY STREET.

9. An actual controversy exists between Plaintiffs and
Defendants relating to their respective rights and duties.

10. Plaintiffs allege and contend:

A. Against all Defendants the more particular facts,
representations and agreements:

(1) That Plaintiffs are the owners in fee simple of
the real property legally described as Lot 1 of Tract 2.

(2) Defendants agreed to:
(a) refinance said first trust deed loan at
2% loan fee at any time.
(b) automatically refinance upon Plaintiffs'
demand.
(c) honor their agreement as consideration for
Plaintiffs' election of EASY STREET

1   SAVINGS AND LOAN's fixed-rate 13% per annum loan

2   (3)   That Plaintiffs are entitled to obtain from De-
3   fendants, and each of them, a loan of any size up to $240,000.00
4   or any principal balance with payment monthly of principal and
5   interest of $2,214.28 or less, without additional credit proces-
6   sing or charges, as Plaintiffs are and were already paying
7   $2,214.28 per month on established credit and loan in place on
8   subject real property.

9   (4)   That Plaintiffs are entitled to obtain refinance
10 from Defendants at total loan fee of 2% of new loan principal bal-
11 ance, without additional fees or charges, whatsoever.

12   (5)   That no re-appraisal is necessary, no appraisal
13 fee to be paid by Plaintiffs to Defendants, as such bears no rea-
14 sonable relationship to subject real property based upon the
15 previous appraisal and sales price.

16   (6)   That no Prepayment penalty be charged on any
17 refinance nor any subsequent resale of subject real property after
18 refinance of said trust deed loan.

19   (7)   That refinance of subject real property loan
20 be made at competitive interest rate, payment, terms and condi-
21 tions, consistent with contract and representations made to
22 Plaintiffs, supra.

23   B.   That the defendants are estopped from denying the
24 validity of Plaintiffs' contentions.

25   C.   That Plaintiffs face irreparable financial losses
26 by virtue of Defendants' actions and inactions.

27   D.   Plaintiffs are informed and believe and thereupon
28 allege that the Defendants admit Plaintiffs' contentions.

1   11. No adequate remedy, other than herein prayed for, exists
2   by which the rights of the parties hereto may be determined.
3   12. Plaintiffs desire a judicial determination of the
4   rights, duties and obligations of all of the parties and a further
5   determination as to their fees and charges on refinance of subject
6   real property loan at terms and conditions consistent with Plain-
7   tiffs' contractual rights herein.
8   SECOND CAUSE OF ACTION (DECLARATORY RELIEF)
9   13. Plaintiffs incorporate by reference all paragraphs al-
10 leged in this complaint as though fully set forth again herein.
11   14. Defendants threaten to and, unless restrained, will
12 charge excess interest rate, excessive loan fees and charges, un-
13 necessary re-appraisal and fees attached thereto, unnecessary
14 credit report and charges, title reports and policies, prepayment
15 penalties and/or non-assumable loan, and/or failure to extend
16 subject loan amount consistent with the current $2,214.28 monthly
17 payment Plaintiffs are paying.
18   15. Plaintiffs seek determination of their rights to remedy
19 said situation, supra, and obtain refinancing of present first
20 trust deed loan at market interest rates, and on terms and condi-
21 tions promised Plaintiff, supra, on subject real property.
22   THIRD CAUSE OF ACTION (INTERFERENCE WITH ECONOMIC ADVANTAGE)
23   16. Plaintiffs incorporate by reference all paragraphs al-
24 leged in this complaint as though fully set forth again herein.
25   17. Plaintiffs, if not allowed by Defendants, and each of
26 them, to refinance for a principal amount consistent with $2,214.28
27 monthly payment at the agreed 2% loan fee, will be in jeopardy of
28 losing $600.00 per month excessive interest, investment opportuni-

ties, profits, and suffer irreparable damage to present and future
Economic Advantage.

18. By reason of the foregoing, Plaintiffs are entitled to
general damages of $1,000,000.00.

FOURTH CAUSE OF ACTION (EQUITABLE ESTOPPEL)

19. Plaintiffs incorporate by reference all paragraphs alleged in this complaint as though fully set forth again herein.

20. Defendants, and each of them, by reason of the foregoing, are equitably estopped from proceeding on their current course
of conduct and inaction in depriving Plaintiffs of their profita-
bility, savings, and refinance at terms and conditions alleged
herein.

FIFTH CAUSE OF ACTION (CONSTRUCTIVE TRUST)

21. Plaintiffs incorporate by reference all paragraphs alleged in this complaint as though fully set forth again herein.

22. By reason of the facts hereinabove set forth and the
confidential and fiduciary relationship between the Plaintiffs and
Defendants, said Defendants, and each of them, are the involuntary
trustees of the excessive interest rate charges on said real property loan since October 23, 1986.

SIXTH CAUSE OF ACTION (QUIET TITLE)

23. Plaintiffs incorporate by reference all paragraphs alleged in this complaint as though fully set forth again herein.

24. Plaintiffs claim that Defendants continuing to hold a
Note secured by Deed of Trust at 13% interest per annum is a cloud
on title to the extent that said interest rate exceeds market
interest rate demanded by Plaintifff consistent with terms and
supra represented to Plaintiffs, supra.

1   SEVENTH CAUSE OF ACTION (BREACH OF FIDUCIARY DUTY)

2   25. Plaintiffs incorporate by reference all paragraphs al-

3 leged in this complaint as though fully set forth again herein.

4   26. That a fiduciary and trust relationship exists between

5 Plaintiffs and Defendants and that Defendants actions and inaction

6 to refinance said real property on terms and conditions, supra, has

7 breached this relationship.

8   27. By reason of the foregoing, Plaintiffs have suffered

9 general damages in the sum of $1,000,000.00.

10   EIGHTH CAUSE OF ACTION (PROMISSORY ESTOPPEL)

11   28. Plaintiffs incorporate by reference all Paragraphs al-

12 leged in this complaint as though fully set forth again herein.

13   29. That by reason of Plaintiffs' action in obtaining said

14 first trust deed loan from EASY STREET through Defendants, and

15 each of the, as aforestated in reliance upon Defendants' promises

16 and agreements, supra, Defendants are estopped from asserting any

17 rights to loan fees in excess of 2% of refinanced principal at any

18 time herein alleged.

19   NINTH CAUSE OF ACTION (BAD FAITH)

20   30. Plaintiffs incorporate by reference all paragraphs al-

21 leged in this complaint as though fully set forth again herein.

22   31. By reason of the foregoing, all Defendants inclusive,

23 engaged in bad faith through financing the afore-described real

24 property in the manner depicted supra and Defendants subsequent

25 refusal to honor the agreed refinance terms.

26   32. Defendants and each of them engaged in additional acts

27 of bad faith by quoting and charging loan fees and conditions

28 which Defendants, and each of them, know are totally unnecessary,

excessive, and improper; and bear no reasonable relationship to
protecting Defendant EASY STREET's security interest in subject
real property. Defendants, and each of them, intentionally have
violated loan policy and Plaintiffs' contractual rights by asserting loan requirements which have no logical relationship to an
existing trustor and property secured. Defendants' conduct and
purported charges is solely designed for the exclusive financial
benefit of Defendants, and each of them, to the exclusion of Plaintiff's rights.

33. By reason of the foregoing, Plaintiffs are entitled to
Bad Faith damages in the sum of $2,000,000.00.

TENTH CAUSE OF ACTION (BREACH OF WARRANTY)

34. Plaintiffs incorporate by reference all Paragraphs alleged in this complaint as though fully set forth again herein.

35. That Defendants, and each of them, represented to Plaintiffs as alleged supra as to refinancing said real property loan
on subject real property.

36. These representations were not true and were not performed by Defendants and each of them.

37. By reason of the foregoing, Plaintiffs are entitled to
general damages in the sum of $1,000,000.00.

ELEVENTH CAUSE OF ACTION (BREACH OF CONTRACT)

38. Plaintiffs incorporate by reference all Paragraphs alleged in this complaint as though fully set forth again herein.

39. Plaintiffs performed all conditions of the above-stated
contract and loan with EASY STREET SAVINGS AND LOAN ASSOCIATION,
relating to subject real property described supra.

40. Defendants, and each of them, failed and refused to

perform pursuant to said contract and loan refinance agreements
and representations herein.

41. By reason of the foregoing, Plaintiffs were required to
engage the services of licensed attorney, who is entitled to attorneys' fees for the value of his services in connection with this
lawsuit.

42. Plaintiffs will suffer special damages in the sum of
approximately $600.00 per month, or more, excess interest per month
from October 23, 1986, loss of profits and interest on said excess
interest being paid presently and in the future, plus an unknown
amount of refinance charges and fees in the future.

43. Plaintiffs have suffered general damages, by reason of
the foregoing, in the sum of $1,000,000.00.

TWELFTH CAUSE OF ACTION (FRAUD)

44. Plaintiffs incorporate by reference all Paragraphs alleged in this complaint as though fully set forth again herein.

45. Defendants, and each of them, represented to Plaintiffs,
supra.

46. Plaintiffs relied upon the aforestated misrepresentations to their detriment.

47. That by reason of the foregoing, said Defendants, and
each of them, either intentionally or maliciously, or in conscious
disregard of the consequences of their actions and/or the actions
of their agents, permitted said conduct to occur without disclosure to Plaintiffs. By reason thereof, Plaintiffs are entitled to
$2,000,000.00 punitive damages against said Defendants, and each
of them.

//   //

1

THIRTEENTH CAUSE OF ACTION (NEGLIGENCE)

2   48. Plaintiffs incorporate by reference all Paragraphs al-

3 leged in this complaint as though fully set forth again herein.

4   49. Defendants, and each of them, failed to advise, protect,

5 disclose, or perform their obligations to Plaintiffs herein.

6   50. That Defendants, and each of them, negligently, care-

7 lessly and unskillfully handled the aforesaid transactions by

8 their actions and omissions, proximately causing losses and

9 damages to Plaintiffs.

10   51. By reason of the foregoing, Plaintiffs are entitled to

11 general damages in the sum of $1,000,000.00.

12 FOURTEENTH CAUSE OF ACTION (INFLICTION OF EMOTIONAL DISTRESS)

13   52. Plaintiffs incorporate by reference all Paragraphs al-

14 leged in this complaint as though fully set forth again herein.

15   53. The aforedescribed conduct of the Defendants, and each

16 of them, was and is outrageous.

17   54. Defendants, and each of them, knew, or should have known,

18 that the aforedescribed conduct intentionally or is substantially

19 certain to cause excessive worry, stress and emotional distress

20 and/or negligently permitted their agents to be in position to

21 aggravate the preexisting circumstances.

22   55. By reason of the foregoing, Plaintiffs are entitled to

23 $1,000,000.00 general damages.

24   FIFTEENTH CAUSE OF ACTION (CONFLICT OF INTEREST)

25   56. Plaintiffs incorporate by reference all Paragraphs al-

26 leged in this complaint as though fully set forth again herein.

27   57. Defendants, and each of them, knowingly gained an ad-

28 vantage to the disadvantage of Plaintiffs, without Plaintiffs'

knowledge, in the financing of Plaintiffs' real property. This
conduct represented a Conflict of Interest.

58. By reason of the foregoing, Plaintiffs are entitled to
general damages in the sum of $1,000,000.00.

SIXTEENTH CAUSE OF ACTION (FAILURE OF FAIR DEALING)

59. Plaintiffs incorporate by reference all Paragraphs alleged in this complaint as though fully set forth again herein.

60. Defendants' aforestated conduct constitutes a Failure
of Fair Dealing with Plaintiffs and is a violation of contractual
and tortious rights Plaintiffs expected from contractual relationships with Defendants, and had reason to expect in the future.

61. By reason of this conduct, Plaintiffs are entitled to
general damages in the sum of $2,000,000.00.

SEVENTEENTH CAUSE OF ACTION (ACCOUNTING)

62. Plaintiffs incorporate by reference all Paragraphs alleged in this complaint as though fully set forth again herein.

63. Defendants, and each of the, are obligated, and Plaintiffs are entitled to an accounting of all funds paid Defendants,
or each of them, for principal and interest, since October 23,
1986, PLUS all excess interest paid since said date of attempted
refinance by Plaintiffs.

EIGHTEENTH CAUSE OF ACTION (UNJUST ENRICHMENT)

64. Plaintiffs incorporate by reference all Paragraphs alleges in this complaint as though fully set forth again herein.

65. By reason of the foregoing, Defendants, and each of
them, have been unjustly enriched by their conduct and omissions
toward Plaintiffs in regard to benefitting Defendants exclusively,
to the exclusion of Plaintiffs' interests.

1   66. By reason of this conduct, Plaintiffs are entitled to
2 all sums Defendants have wrongfully gained, in addition to general
3 damages of $1,000,000.00.

4   NINETEENTH CAUSE OF ACTION (REFORMATION)

5   67. Plaintiffs incorporate by reference all Paragraphs al-
6 leged in this complaint as though fully set forth again herein.

7   68. By reason of the foregoing, Plaintiffs are entitled to
8 REFORMATION of the Note and Deed of Trust with EASY STREET SAVINGS
9 AND LOAN ASSOCIATION from the interest rates charged, and princi-
10 pal balance thereof, to market lower interest rates and an in-
11 creased principal balance within the existing monthly payment of
12 $2,214.57.

13   WHEREFORE, Plaintiffs pray for Judgment against the Defen-
14 dants, and each of them, as follows:

15   1. For an order requiring Defendants to show cause, if any
16 they have, why they should not be enjoined as hereinafter set
17 forth during the pendency of this action;

18   2. A temporary restraining order, preliminary injunction,
19 and final injunction issue restraining the Defendants, their
20 agents, attorneys, and representatives, and all persons in active
21 concert or participation with them, from continuing to charge
22 13% interest per annum on subject real property loan by EASY
23 STREET SAVINGS AND LOAN ASSOCIATION on loan number RU 1234 on the
24 real property owned in fee simple by Plaintiffs, legally described
25 as Lot 1 of Tract 2, Los Angeles, Los Angeles County, State of
26 California, commonly described as 888 Rough Road, Los Angeles;
27 and additionally, requiring Defendants, and each of them, to re-
28 duce the 13% interest per annum to market interest rate hereafter

at the maximum principal amount payable at $2,214.57 per month
on a 30 year fixed rate fully amortized real property loan;

3. Declaring the rights and duties of the parties;

4. GENERAL DAMAGES in the sum of $1,000,000.00;

5. BAD FAITH and UNFAIR DEALING damages in the sum of
$2,000,000.00;

6. PUNITIVE DAMAGES for FRAUD in the sum of $2,000,000.00;

7. SPECIAL DAMAGES:

   (1) Excess interest of $600, or more, per month on
        existing loan;
   (2) Loss of interest and profits from October 23, 1986
        on excess interest;
   (3) Refinance charges and fees according to proof on
        subject loan;
   (4) Other special expenses, according to proof;

8. Attorneys fees, according to proof;

9. For an ACCOUNTING of all interest and principal paid;

10. For REFORMATION of loan trust deed and note with
EASY STREET SAVINGS AND LOAN;

11. Court costs; and

12. Such other and further relief as the Court deems just.

DATED: JANUARY 5, 1987

                                   _____
                                   MICHAEL D. HILLER
                                   Attorney for Plaintiffs

COMMENTARY ON COMPLAINT #1

I will take you through the long Complaint.

First are the "form" paragraphs. "DOE" clauses for individuals, partnerships, and corporations, are fictitious parties. You may not know their identity at the outset. This clause gives an opportunity to amend the complaint if and when unnamed parties are discovered in the case. Without a DOE clause, you would need Court permission to add named Defendants later.

Paragraph 4 is a "Mutual Agency" clause. It enables you to generally lump all defendants together in avoiding long allegations of individual relationships among Defendants.

The First Cause of Action is crucial to your case. It is equitable or injunctive relief for your NMA. Paragraph 11 alleges that there is "no adequate remedy at law."

You tackle your relief both ways, money and/or an NMA. $7,200 x 25 years = $180,000. This is adequate for out of pocket or special damages.

Seeking a Temporary Restraining Order, Preliminary Injunction and Permanent Injunction confers equitable jurisdiction upon the court to impose affirmatively an NMA.

A court usually imposes negative relief by denying the right or permission to do something. The prayer demands that the court deny the lender the continuation of 13% interest by allowing only 10%, or the market interest rate.

Declaratory Relief is a secondary way to impose equitable relief. It states, as a legal conclusion, that a stated condition exists. In effect, you are seeking to be declared the winner of an NMA.

Interference with Economic Advantage is an important new tort which establishes damages. It is not quite fraud, but more than simple breach of contract.

Equitable Estoppel and Constructive Trust are equitable theories which require Defendants to hold ill-gotten gains for Plaintiffs' benefit.

Quiet Title is usually to remove an adverse claim which clouds title to real property. This theory is used here, as a novel approach, where lender's excessive interest impairs salability.

Breach of Fiduciary Duty imposes a high ethical, moral, and legal responsibility upon professionals dealing with clients. It requires higher than average care in trust relationships. Certain categories of people rely upon the expertise of the specialist to protect their interests.

Promissory Estoppel is a bar to anyone taking advantage of a promise which others rely on justifiably. It is a substitute for consideration in a contract.

Bad Faith is also known, in California, as Breach of the Implied Covenant of Good Faith and Fair Dealing (16th Cause of Action). It is now an unwritten condition of any Contract.

Breach of Warranty often includes the same promises included in the Breach of Contract action. This count covers the type of express or implied promise relied upon as a guarantee.

Breach of Contract requires an offer and acceptance, consideration, and performance. Plaintiffs must also perform their side of the bargain to qualify to sue the other party to the transaction. Where the contract provides for attorney's fees, California law requires them to be reciprocal, to the prevailing party.

Fraud requires specific representations, either false or to deliberately mislead, without intention of performing. Punitive damages are permitted to punish the wrongdoer. These damages may be nominal—as small as $1.00, or huge—millions of dollars. Important factors in determining the size of the award are:

(a) the outrageousness of the conduct; and

(b) the net worth of the Defendant.

Negligence requires carelessness by a party to a transaction in order to impose liability. It is composed of a duty to the injured party, a breach of said duty, and injury or damages proximately caused thereby.

The standard of care is the norm for the industry, average care. In law school we learned the term "TARM", The Average Reasonable Man test. In real estate, I prefer "TARB", The Average Reasonable Broker.

You can invent your own alphabet description. The Average Reasonable Escrow is "TARE"; The Average Reasonable Seller is "TARS," et cetera.

Infliction of Emotional Distress is an overlooked factor in many business transactions. Isn't it amazing how money makes us upset? It seems to have a stranglehold on our emotions. "Outrageous conduct" is a key element of this tort. Foreseeability of the effect on you is also important in the determination of the outrage.

Conflict of Interest is not yet a recognized tort

in California. However, new torts may be created by legislative action or subsequently recognized by case decisions. It is akin to Breach of Fiduciary Duty but covers areas where there may not be a Fiduciary Relationship. An unfair, self-serving situation arises where one party to a transaction has a secret agenda to quietly take advantage of another's trust and confidence. This should be remedied.

Unfair Dealing can be combined with Bad Faith or with its cousin—Breach of Implied Covenant of Good Faith.

Accounting has a useful purpose where you are entitled to a rebate for excessive payments made before the case gets to trial.

Unjust Enrichment is a catchall theory where one party is unfairly benefitted, to the detriment of the other.

Reformation is tantamount to judicial rewriting of your Promissory Note into an NMA. It changes the contract terms to what your lender has refused to do, but to which you are equitably entitled.

WHEREFORE is the "Prayer" for relief in your lawsuit. Notice that the General and Punitive Damages are seven figures. Don't get married to these numbers. Asking prices are not necessarily selling prices. You have to "prove" your damages by a "Preponderence" of the evidence. You also need to prove that you are entitled to each element establishing your case by more than one-half the believable evidence.

The most important reason to ask a large amount for damages is to avoid making a Court Motion for an increase in monetary damages. You may also request General or Punitive Damages, "according to proof." Show the Defendants that you are serious and mean business.

Law Offices of
MICHAEL D. HILLER
16055 Ventura Boulevard
Suite 603
Encino, CA 91436
Telephone: (818) 990-7843

Attorney for Plaintiffs

SUPERIOR COURT OF THE STATE OF CALIFORNIA

FOR THE COUNTY OF LOS ANGELES

I.M. VICTIM and MAY BEE) CASE NO.
VICTIM,   )
) COMPLAINT FOR:
            Plaintiffs,)
) 1. TEMPORARY RESTRAINING ORDER
vs.   )   AND PERMANENT INJUNCTIONS
) 2. INTERFERENCE WITH ECONOMIC
EASY STREET SAVINGS AND)   ADVANTAGE
LOAN ASSOCIATION, a Cali-) 3. BREACH OF CONTRACT
fornia Corporation; DOES) 4. FRAUD
1 to 200, inclusive; DOE) 5. NEGLIGENCE
CORPORATIONS 1 to 200;   ) 6. REFORMATION
inclusive; DOE PARTNER-)
SHIPS 1 to 200, inclu-   )
sive,   )
            Defendants.)
_____)

PLAINTIFFS ALLEGE:

FIRST CAUSE OF ACTION

TEMPORARY RESTRAINING ORDER AND PERMANENT INJUNCTIONS

   1. At all times herein mentioned the Plaintiffs and Defendants were residents of the County of Los Angeles, State of California.

   2. (a) At all times mentioned herein, Defendants EASY
STREET SAVINGS AND LOAN ASSOCIATION, DOE CORPORATIONS 1 to 200,
inclusive, were California corporations, organized and existing

1 under the laws of the State of California.

2   (b) DOE PARTNERSHIPS 1 to 200, inclusive, are Partner-
3 ships, organized and existing under the laws of the State of Cali-
4 fornia.

5   3. The true names and capacities, whether individual, cor-
6 porate, associate, or otherwise of Defendants named herein as DOES
7 1 to 200, inclusive; DOE CORPORATIONS 1 to 200, inclusive; DOE
8 PARTNERSHIPS 1 to 200, inclusive, are unknown to Plaintiffs, who
9 therefore sue said Defendants by such fictitious names and Plain-
10 tiffs will ask leave to amend this Complaint to show their true
11 names and capacities when the same has been ascertained.

12   4. At all times herein mentioned, the Defendants, and each
13 of them, were the agents, employees and employers of each of their
14 co-defendants and in doing the things hereinafter alleged, were
15 acting within the course and scope of said agency and employment
16 with consent and knowledge of each other.

17   5. On October 23, 1981, Plaintiffs became the legal owners
18 of the real property legally described as Lot 1 of Tract 2, as per
19 Map recorded in Book 3 page 4, parcel 5, in Los Angeles, County
20 of Los Angeles, State of California, commonly described as 888
21 Rough Street.

22   6. Defendant EASY STREET SAVINGS AND LOAN ASSOCIATION, de-
23 fendants, and each of them, loaned $200,000.00 to Plaintiffs on a
24 30 year fully amortized fixed-rate loan, payable $2,214.57 per
25 month at 13% per annum, secured by a Note and Deed of Trust on
26 subject real property supra.

27   Plaintiffs obtained said loan on the express representations
28 by Defendants, and each of them, that the loan could be refinanced

1 at any time thereafter, for a one-time loan fee of 2% of the prin-
2 cipal balance, whenever the interest rates became lower than 13%
3 per annum.

4   Plaintiffs became Trustors and EASY STREET, the beneficiary
5 of subject real property loan on a fixed rate of 13% on the re-
6 finance representation of 2% loan fee, with no additional charges
7 or costs.

8   7. On October 23, 1986, Plaintiffs approached EASY STREET
9 to refinance said loan, when said loan had a principal balance of
10 approximately $195,000.00 and market loan rates for single family
11 residences, such as Plaintiffs', was at or under 10% per annum,
12 for 30 year fixed-rate loans. At said time, Defendants, and each
13 of them quoted 10% per annum fixed rate loan with 2% loan fee plus
14 $350.00 appraisal fee, credit check charges, $400 escrow fees, and
15 various other charges which were unnecessary and unwarranted for
16 said refinance.

17   Plaintiffs learned that 10% per annum interest rate would re-
18 sult in a monthly savings of approximately $600.00. Despite a
19 lower payment by a refinance at lower interest rates, Defendants,
20 and each of them, demanded a credit report and application to be
21 prepared and paid for by Plaintiffs and a reappraisal of subject
22 real property, to be paid for by Plaintiffs.

23   Defendants, and each of them, approved Plaintiffs credit for
24 $2,214.28 monthly payment in October, 1981 when subject property
25 was appraised and was purchased by Plaintiffs for $320,000.00

26   8. Defendants' attempts to enforce refinance loan fees of 2%
27 plus appraisal, credit, escrow, title policy, and other various
28 fees and charges, with or without additional loan proceeds, places

1 an unnecessary and unwarranted financial burden and economic

2 duress on Plaintiffs, contrary to the contractual agreements and

3 assurances Plaintiff received when obtaining said loan from EASY

4 STREET.

5   9. An actual controversy exists between Plaintiffs and De-

6 fendants relating to their respective rights and duties.

7   10. Plaintiffs allege and contend:

8   A. Against all Defendants the more particular facts, re-

9 presentations and agreements:

10   (1) That Plaintiffs are the owners in fee simple of

11 the real property legally described as Lot 1 Tract 2, commonly

12 described as 888 Rough Road, Los Angeles, California.

13   (2) Defendants agreed to:

14   (a) refinance said first trust deed loan at 1%
                             loan fee at any time.
15   (b) automatically refinance upon Plaintiffs'
                             demand.
16   (c) honor their agreement as consideration
                             for Plaintiffs' election of Defendant EASY
17   STREET's fixed rate 13% per annum loan.

18   (3) That Plaintiffs are entitled to obtain from De-

19 fendants, and each of them, a Note Modification Agreement on a

20 principal balance of $200,000.00 with a monthly payment of princi-

21 pal and interest of $1614.00, without additional credit processing

22 or charges, as Plaintiffs are and were already paying $2214.28 per

23 month on established credit and loan in place on subject real pro-

24 perty.

25   (4) That Plaintiffs are entitled to obtain refinance

26 from Defendants at a total loan fee of 2% of new loan principal

27 balance, without additional fees or charges, whatsoever.

28   (5) That no re-appraisal is necessary nor appraisal

fee to be paid by Plaintiffs to Defendants, as such bears no rational nor reasonable relationship to subject real property based upon the previous appraisal and sales price.

B. That the defendants are estopped from denying the validity of Plaintiffs' contentions.

C. That Plaintiffs face irreparable financial losses by virtue of Defendants actions and inactions.

D. Plaintiffs are informed and believe and thereupon allege that the Defendants admit Plaintiffs' contentions.

11. No adequate remedy, other than herein prayed for, exists by which the rights of the parties hereto may be determined.

12. Plaintiffs desire a judicial determination of the rights, duties and obligations of all the parties and a further determination as to their fees and charges on refinance of subject real property loan at terms and conditons consistent with Plaintiffs' contractual rights herein.

SECOND CAUSE OF ACTION (INTERFERENCE WITH ECONOMIC ADVANTAGE)

13. Plaintiffs incorporate by reference all paragraphs alleged in this complaint as though fully set forth again herein.

14. Plaintiffs, if not allowed by Defendants, and each of them, to refinance by a Note Modification Agreement on $195,000.00 principal balance and a monthly payment of $1614.00 at the agreed 2% loan fee, will be in jeopardy of losing $600.00 per month excessive interest, investment opportunities, profits, and suffer irreparable damage to present and future Economic Advantage.

15. By reason of the foregoing, Plaintiffs are entitled to general damages of $1,000,000.00.

//   //

<u>THIRD CAUSE OF ACTION</u> (BREACH OF CONTRACT)

16. Plaintiffs incorporate by reference all Paragraphs alleged in this complaint as though fully set forth again herein.

17. Plaintiffs performed all conditions of the above-stated contract and loan with EASY STREET SAVINGS AND LOAN ASSOCIATION, relating to subject real property described supra.

18. Defendants, and each of them, failed and refused to perform pursuant to said contract and loan refinance agreements and representations herein.

19. By reason of the foregoing, Plaintiffs were required to engage the services of a licensed attorney, who is entitled to attorneys' fees for the value of his services in connection with this lawsuit.

20. Plaintiffs will suffer special damages in the sum of approximately $600.00 per month, or more excess interest per month from October 23, 1986, loss of profits and interest on said interest being paid presently and in the future, plus an unknown amount of refinance charges and fees in the future.

21. Plaintiffs have suffered general damages by reason of the foregoing, in the sum of $1,000,000.00.

<u>FOURTH CAUSE OF ACTION</u> (FRAUD)

22. Plaintiffs incorporate by reference all Paragraphs alleged in this complaint as though fully set forth again herein.

23. Defendants, and each of them, represented to Plaintiffs supra.

24. Plaintiffs relied upon the aforestated misrepresentations to their detriment.

25. That by reason of the foregoing, said Defendants, and

each of them, either intentionally or maliciously, or in conscious disregard of the consequences of their actions and/or the actions of their agents, permitted said conduct to occur without disclosure to Plaintiffs. By reason thereof, Plaintiffs are entitled to $1,000,000.00 punitive damages against said Defendants, and each of them.

FIFTH CAUSE OF ACTION (NEGLIGENCE)

26. Plaintiffs incorporate by reference all Paragraphs alleged in this complaint as though fully set forth again herein.

27. Defendants, and each of them, failed to advise, protect, disclose, or perform their obligations to Plaintiffs herein.

28. That Defendants, and each of them, negligently, carelessly and unskillfully handled the aforesaid transactions by their actions and omissions, which proximately caused loss and damages to Plaintiffs.

29. By reason of the foregoing, Plaintiffs are entitled to general damages in the sum of $1,000,000.00.

SIXTH CAUSE OF ACTION (REFORMATION)

30. Plaintiffs incorporate by reference all Paragraphs alleged in this complaint as though fully set forth again herein.

31. By reason of the foregoing, Plaintiffs are entitled to REFORMATION of the Note and Deed of Trust with EASY STREET SAVINGS AND LOAN ASSOCIATION by a Note Modification Agreement from 13% interest and $2214.28 monthly payment to a 10% fixed interest rate per annum and a payment of $1,614.00.

WHEREFORE, Plaintiffs pray for Judgment against the Defendants, and each of them, as follows:

1. For an order requiring Defendants to show cause, if any

they have, why they should not be enjoined as hereinafter set
forth during the pendency of this action;

2. A temporary restraining order, preliminary injunction,
and final injunction issue restraining the Defendants, their
agents, attorneys, and representatives, and all persons in active
concert or participation with them, from continuing to charge 13%
interest per annum on subject real property loan by EASY STREET
SAVINGS AND LOAN ASSOCIATION on loan number RU 1234 on the real
property owned in fee simple by Plaintiffs, legally described as
Lot 1 of Tract 2, commonly described as 888 ROUGH ROAD, Los
Angeles, Los Angeles County, State of California; and additionally,
requiring Defendants, and each of them, to execute a Note Modification Agreement to 10% interest rate hereafter payable at $1614
per month on a 25 year fixed rate fully amortized real property
loan;

3. Declaring the rights and duties of the parties;

4. GENERAL DAMAGES in the sum of $1,000,000.00;

5. PUNITIVE DAMAGES for FRAUD in the sum of $2,000,000.00;

6. SPECIAL DAMAGES:
   (1) Excess interest of $600.00, or more, per month on
       existing loan;
   (2) Loss of interest and profits from October 23, 1986
       on excess interest;
   (3) Refinance charges and fees according to proof on
       loan;
   (4) Other special expenses, according to proof;

7. Attorneys fees, according to proof;

8. For REFORMATION of loan trust deed and note with EASY
STREET SAVINGS AND LOAN BY NOTE MODIFICATION AGREEMENT.

9. Court costs; and

10. Such other and further relief as the Court deems just.

DATED: JANUARY 5, 1987

                                _____
                                MICHAEL D. HILLER
                                Attorney for Plaintiffs

COMMENTARY ON SHORT COMPLAINT

Your thrust in this Complaint is for an NMA only. There is no catchall Prayer for new funds here.

The Economic Advantage theory illustrates how devastating $600 a month is to your profit potential. Multiply $7,200 yearly loss to a full 25 year term for a dramatic $180,000 pocketbook loss. This rings the bell at trial as to how much of your money is taken by continuing to pay interest rates above current market.

The theme in this Complaint is straight forward. You seek Reformation of your Note to an NMA or, alternatively, damages on the other legal theories.

21

Following are two model forms which can be used in settlement of lawsuits on real estate issues.

The "Settlement and Release Agreement" covers the settlement of a Prepayment Penalty by a refund of one-half of the interest charged for an early loan payoff.

The "Release" provides for settlement by reference to a Note Modification Agreement and Prepayment penalty.

Both documents have a release of all claims and specifically waives California Civil Code Section 1542 to release unknown claims.

SETTLEMENT AND RELEASE AGREEMENT

This Settlement and Release Agreement ("Agreement") is entered into by and among I.M. VICTIM and MAY BEE VICTIM (collectively "VICTIM") and EASY STREET SAVINGS AND LOAN ASSOCIATION ("EASY STREET") with reference to the following:

On or about October 23, 1981 VICTIM purchased a single family home at 888 Rough Road, Los Angeles, California and financed the purchase in part with a loan from EASY STREET in the amount of $200,000.00 ("Loan Number RU 1234").

Loan Number RU 1234 was evidenced by a Promissory Note ("Note") which contained a provision for a twelve-month prepayment fee in the event VICTIM elected to pay the Note prior to maturity.

On or about June 25, 1985 VICTIM prepaid the Note and EASY STREET collected from VICTIM a prepayment fee in the amount of

On January 15, 1986 VICTIM Filed Complaint Number XYZ 4321 in the Superior Court of the State of California for the County of Los Angeles allegeing, inter alia, that EASY STREET breached the terms of the Note by charging a prepayment fee of   . EASY STREET denies that the prepayment fee was improperly charged or collected.

VICTIM and EASY STREET wish to resolve the dispute without the necessity of time-consuming and expensive litigation.

Therefore, for good and valuable consideration, the receipt and sufficiency of which is hereby acknowledge, VICTIM and EASY STREET agree as follows:

1. EASY STREET will, concurrently with the execution of of this Agreement, refund to VICTIM the sum of which is one-half of the prepayment fee collected by EASY STREET when VICTIM prepaid the Note.

2. VICTIM will cause its attorney, MICHAEL D. HILLER, to file with the Superior Court of Los Angeles, a Dismissal with Prejudice of Case Number XYZ 4321.

3. VICTIM hereby releases EASY STREET, its officers, directors, employees, agents, successors and assigns from any and all claims, demands, obligations of any kind whatsoever, costs, expenses, actions and causes of actions of every nature, character and description, known and unknown, which VICTIM may have against EASY STREET connected with, related to, or arising out of Loan Number RU 1234 referenced previously.

4. VICTIM also waives and relinquishes all rights and benefits afforded by Section 1542 of the California Civil Code which provides that:

"A general release does not extend to claims which the creditor does not know or suspect to exist in his favor at the time of executing the release, which if known by him must of materially affected his settlement with the debtor."

5. This Agreement is a compromise of the disputed claim referenced above and is not to be considered in any way an admission of liability of any party for any purpose.

6. The prevailing party in any action or preceding between VICTIM and EASY STREET relating to this Agreement shall be entitled to receive from the other its costs and reasonable attorney's fees.

Dated:_____

By:_____
    I.M. VICTIM

By:_____
    MAY BEE VICTUM

Dated: September 5, 1986

EASY STREET SAVINGS AND LOAN ASSOCIATION

By: _____
    C.U. SMILING
    Counsel

By: _____
    R.U. HAPPY
    Senior Counsel

<u>RELEASE</u>

WHEREAS on October 23, 1986 I.M. VICTIM and MAY BEE VICTIM (hereinafter "VICTIM") informed EASY STREET SAVINGS AND LOAN ASSOCIATION, A California Corporation (hereinafter "EASY STREET") of their claim which alleged, among other matters, that their loan should not contain a prepayment penalty and not be 13%; and

WHEREAS, the records of EASY STREET reflect that VICTIM purchased that certain parcel of real property and obtained a loan which provided for a 13.00% Interest Rate; and that they executed documents setting forth the terms of the interest rate; and

WHEREAS, VICTIM and EASY STREET have entered into a Note Modification Agreement, a copy of which is attached hereto marked Exhibit "A" and incorporated herein by reference;

NOW, THEREFORE:

For good and valuable consideration, receipt of which is hereby acknowledge, the undersinged hereby release and discharge the persons named below, individually and collectively, from any and all claims, demands and causes of action of whatever kind of nature, whether known or unknown, suspected or unsuspected by me which the undersigned now own or have at any time heretofore owned or held as against the below named persons or any of them, including but not limited to any and all claims, demands or causes of action arising out of or in any way connected with the aforesaid claim any transaction otherwise involving Loan No. RU 1234.

The below named persons who are expressly released and discharged by this document are the following:

EASY STREET SAVINGS AND LOAN ASSOCIATION, A California corporation, its parent, successors in interest, subsidiaries and affiliates, and its officers, employees, directors and trustees.

It is the undersigned's intention in executing this release that the same shall be effective as a bar to each and every claim, demand and cause of action hereinabove specified and in furtherance of this intention the undersigned hereby expressly waive any and all rights and benefits conferred by the provissions of Sections 1542 of the Civil Code of the State of California, which reads:

> "A general release does not extend to claims which the creditor does not know or suspect to exist in his favor at the time of executing the release, which if known by him must have materially affected his settlement with the debtor."

The undersigned expressly consent that this release shall be given full force and effect as to all of its terms and provisions including as well those relating to unsuspected claims, demands and causes or causes of action hereinabove specified. If any provision of this release be invalid or unenforceable, it is the undersigned's intention that all of the other provisions shall be fully valid and enforceable according to their terms.

Dated: This __8th__ day of January, 1987.

_____

I.M. VICTIM

_____

MAY BEE VICTIM

22

General rules and strategies, to impose your own individual justice, aren't enough.

We need mandated legislative action to force compliance with an elemental bit of equity. There must be an undeniable right to refinance existing loans at market interest rates, without unnecessary fees or delays.

How do we get automatically, and immediately, what we now need to fight for?

Everyone in the identical situation must be treated the same. There shouldn't be any disparity between policies of one lender from another. The barrier has to be removed between lender and borrower. It cannot be whatever one party wants to impose upon another.

You would think that progressive, consumer minded legislators would ease the red tape in enforcing an NMA or a similar procedure. Let's avoid the hassle, the specious excuses, the delays, and the phony denials of lowered interest.

My experience with the champions of the people is that they are buffeted by too many special interests. You need your foot in the door to get their ear.

Your goal is to have enough time to present your viewpoint. Because of money, the PACs (Political Action Committees) are effective in getting a foot in the door.

As one famous California political leader once said, "Money is the mother's milk of politics."

It's a sad commentary on how creative, idealistic, hard working representatives of the people get their inspiration to introduce new laws and change old laws.

An extreme example of legislators' reliance upon input from their constituents was the SST.

The Supersonic Transport was defeated by one vote in the United States Senate in 1974. Why? Due to a "deluge" of 29 letters received by one Senator, casting the deciding vote in opposition to an American built plane. An inference is drawn from a vocal sampling as to how the majority are thinking on a particular issue.

The bottom line is to get political influence. You need to know an Assemblyman or State Senator personally.

Get an introduction or personal audience. Give a significant political campaign contribution. Get a letter writing campaign started. Write an initiative.

That is why we need you to circulate and sign the petition that you will find at the end of this book. Xeroxed copies will also work. Signed petitions on the desk of your legislator will be weighed. They probably will not be read. The weight on the scales of justice may depend on the weight of the results of our grass roots campaign for equality to negotiate fair contracts with the lender.

Strength in numbers will get the results for consumers. The best way to get the ear, attention, and responsiveness of the politician is for us to band together in asserting the will of the public.

Let your elected representative know that there are huge numbers of voters watching and waiting to see what will be done to solve the need for fair, fast, and favorable financing.

ACCELERATION CLAUSE: **A contract provision providing for the entire loan principal to become immediately due and payable upon the happening of a specific condition or event.**

ACCOUNTING: **A detailed statement of the mutual demands of debt and credit between the parties arising out of contract or fiduciary relationship.**

ACCRUED INTEREST: **Interest which has been deferred beyond the period earned.**

ADHESION CONTRACT: **A one-sided contract without equality of bargaining position where a standard contract term is forced upon the second party, to its** *detriment. Said contract term or provision may not be specifically enforceable if unconscionable.*

AMORTIZATION TABLE: *A schedule for a complete payoff of a certain sum and interest in a given period by scheduled payments over the term.*

ANSWER: *Defendant's pleading contesting Plaintiff's complaint/lawsuit.*

APPRAISAL: *An estimate of value.*

ASSUMABLE LOAN: *A loan which can be transferred, upon its original terms, to a new owner.*

ASSUMPTION FEE: *A charge by the lender to substitute loan debtors on the original loan made, by relieving the first borrower of liability.*

BAD FAITH: *Actual or constructive fraud by secretly misleading another, intentionally refusing to fulfill an obligation.*

BASIS POINTS: *1/100 of 1% as additional interest chargeable on a loan.*

BENEFICIARY: *Creditor in a Deed of Trust on real property.*

BREACH OF FIDUCIARY DUTY: *Failure to perform to a higher standard of trust and confidence required by a special relationship between the parties.*

BREACH OF WARRANTY: Failure of an express or implied promise that a fact is true.

CAP: The maximum interest percentage changes under a VIR (Variable Interest Rate) loan.

CASH FLOW: The net positive or negative cash return, from an investment, after paying operating expenses and debt service.

CLOSING STATEMENT: Balance sheet at COE itemizing accounting disbursements.

COE: Close of Escrow.

COMPLAINT: The first pleading in a civil action by a Plaintiff starting the lawsuit.

CONFIDENTIALITY CLAUSE: Condition of secrecy to a settlement or release of a claim or lawsuit.

CONFLICT OF INTEREST: Two competing interests which are irreconcilable. (Where one is attempting to serve two masters).

CONSIDERATION: The inducement to a contract; act or forbearance, or promise thereof, in an offer and acceptance between the parties.

CONSTRUCTIVE TRUST: Establishing those holding title or possession to property as trustee(s) for claimant/Plaintiff.

CONTRACT: An agreement, upon sufficient consideration, to do or not to do a particular act.

DECLARATORY RELIEF: Court opinion determining the rights of the parties, or a question of law, without ordering anything to be done.

DEED OF TRUST: A three party real estate encumbrance instrument in which the legal title to the obligation to pay money is in a trustee, with real estate to secure repayment by trustor (borrower) to Beneficiary (creditor).

DEMURRER: A legal pleading which disputes the sufficiency of a Complaint or Cross-Complaint.

DOE: Fictitious party Defendant of a lawsuit.

ECONOMIC DURESS: Forced business choice where there is no freedom of decision, no reasonable alternative.

EMOTIONAL DISTRESS, INFLICTION OF: The tort of intentionally or negligently causing worry, stress, agravation by conduct.

ENCUMBRANCE: A lien, liability, mortgage or Trust Deed on real property.

EQUITABLE ESTOPPEL: Judicially stopping one whose acts, conduct or silence, denies claimed rights to be asserted.

EQUITABLE RELIEF: Result sought on basis of justice and fairness, to impose a benefit for Plaintiff, by imposing conditions of action or inaction upon others.

ESCROW: **A neutral depository and stakeholder which holds and processes documents and funds.**

ESTOPPEL: **Forbidden by law to speak against one's own act or deed.**

FAIR DEALING: **Equitable and honest business practices.**

FHLB: **Federal Home Loan Bank.**

FIDUCIARY: **Holder of trust and confidence for the benefit of another.**

FIRST POSITION: **The most senior lien or encumbrance on real estate title records.**

FORECLOSURE: **The termination of the owner/trustor's interest and rights in the real property covered by the mortgage or trust deed.**

FRAUD: **False representation of fact by words or conduct; intentionally deceiving another, causing damages.**

FUNDING: **The financing, by payment of loan funds, near the close of escrow.**

GENERAL DAMAGES: **Damages implied, or presumed, as a direct result from another's breach or wrong.**

IMPLIED COVENANT OF GOOD FAITH AND FAIR DEALING: **An unwritten part of every California contractual relationship to deal honestly, fairly and in good faith with the other parties thereto.**

INADEQUATE REMEDY AT LAW: **When the relief sought is preventive, rather than compensatory.**

INCORPORATE BY REFERENCE: **To include without repeating.**

INFRA: **Below, after.**

INJUNCTION: **A prohibitive writ, allowing or stopping an act which is unjust and inequitable, which has no adequate remedy in money damages.**

INTERFERENCE WITH ECONOMIC ADVANTAGE: **Conduct which deprives claimant of a business opportunity to earn profits, interest, earnings or money to which claimant is entitled.**

IRREPARABLE DAMAGES: **Damages for which no certain monetary standard exists for measurement.**

LIEN: **A charge, security, or encumbrance upon property.**

LOAN COMMITMENT: **An oral or written promise to process a loan in a limited period of time, usually 30-60 days, at specified interest rate, monthly payment, terms and charges/fees.**

MALICIOUS: **Intentional doing of a wrongful act, to cause damages, without cause.**

M.O.: **Modus operandi; method of operation; scheme.**

MORTGAGE BROKER: **A real estate broker who arran-**

ges secured loans on real estate between lenders and borrowers.

MUTUAL AGENCY: *Catchall (paragraph 4) Complaint allegation, establishing agency and employment relationships between parties Defendant, to a lawsuit, without individually specifying each relationship.*

NEGATIVE AMORTIZATION: *Interest, in excess of monthly payment schedule, requiring an addition to principal balance of the obligation.*

NEGLIGENCE: *Doing, or failing to do, something, which TARM (The Average Reasonable Man) would not do; failing to meet the standard care required by duty to others.*

NMA: *Note Modification Agreement. A contract which modifies an existing Note, secured by a Deed of Trust, on real property.*

OUTRAGEOUS CONDUCT: *A serious insulting or abusive wrong committed to the person, feelings or rights of another.*

P&L STATEMENT: *Profit and Loss Statement.*

PAC: *Political Action Committee.*

POINTS: *The percentage of a loan principal amount charged as a loan fee by lender.*

PRAYER: *Request for relief in a lawsuit (Complaint or Cross-Complaint).*

PRELIMINARY INJUNCTION: An Injunction ordering or restraining conduct until the time of trial.

PREPAYMENT PENALTY: A clause in a Note and/or Deed of Trust, requiring a penalty for early payoff, in part or full, of the principal balance—usually 6 months' interest.

PROMISSORY ESTOPPEL: A promise which is reasonably expected to, and does, induce action or forebearance and is binding, if injustice can be avoided only by enforcement of promise.

PROMISSORY NOTE: A written promise to pay a specified sum at a time certain, or on demand, to a named person or his order.

PROXIMATE CAUSE: The direct cause, producing damage, without which the result would not have occurred.

PUNITIVE DAMAGES: Punishment damages.

QUIET TITLE: Establishing Plaintiff's title to real property by compelling an adverse claimant to establish his claim or be forever barred from asserting it.

RECONVEYANCE: An instrument which is recorded on real estate chain of title when a loan secured by Trust Deed, is paid off in full.

REFINANCE: To obtain a new loan, replacing an original or previous loan on real property.

REFORMATION: Equitable remedy to reform or rewrite contracts which fail, through fraud, mutual mistake, or understanding of the parties, to express the parties' true intention.

RELEASE: Giving up a claim or potential claim.

S.O.P.: Standard Operating Procedure.

SUMMONS: A notice to Defendant or Cross-Defendant that an action has been started and that a judgment will be entered against him if he fails to answer.

SUPRA: Above, before.

TARB: The Average Reasonable Broker.

TARE: The Average Reasonable Escrow.

TARL: The Average Reasonable Lender.

TARM: The Average Reasonable Man.

TARS: The Average Reasonable Seller.

TD: Trust Deed; Deed of Trust.

TITLE: The right to, or ownership in, land; The right to a Cause of Action.

TITLE INSURANCE: Insurance against loss or damage resulting from defects or failure of title to a particular parcel of real estate, or from the enforcement of liens existing against it at the time of the insurance.

TORT: **A civil wrong or injury violating a duty imposed by statutory or case law.**

TRO: **Temporary Restraining Order.**

TRANSFER FEE: **The lender's fee to substitute a new debtor (trustor) on a Deed of Trust.**

TRUSTEE: **One who executes a trust. Enforcer of foreclosure on real property on behalf of Beneficiary.**

TRUSTOR: **One who creates a Trust. Obligor/debtor to a Deed of Trust on real property.**

UNILATERAL: **One-sided.**

UNJUST ENRICHMENT: **Person should not profit inequitably at another's expense.**

VIR: **Variable Interest Rate**

VARIABLE FORMULA: **The conditions which determine the size and frequency of interest rate changes.**

VARIABLE LOAN: **A Note which starts at a fixed rate of interest, but changeable (variable) by its terms, a given increase or decrease in monthly payment and annual interest rate, at specified time periods, upon a set formula.**

MICHAEL D. HILLER

*Michael D. Hiller is a trial lawyer and Real
Estate Broker. He has practiced law since 1962 and has
been a Real Estate Broker since 1959. He has been active
in many civic, service and legal groups in his career.
During his career he has spoken to over 1250
organizations throughout California.*

*He has led Bar Associations as President of
the East Los Angeles Bar in 1966 and the
Los Angeles Trial Lawyers Association in 1980. LATLA is
the largest metropolitan Trial Bar in the world. From
1969 to 1971 he was President of the Los Angeles
Neighborhood Legal Services Society. LANLSS was part
of the War on Poverty and Office
of Economic Opportunity.*

*His activity in the California Trial Lawyers
Association was marked by being Public Information
Officer in 1972, Speaker Bureau Chairman for 3 years,
and Editor-in-chief of the CTLA magazine
"THE FORUM."*

*Michael D. Hiller was host of a weekly radio talk
show on KIEV (870AM). The program, entitled
"Mike Hiller's Real Estate Rights",
emphasized how to avoid legal problems
in the buying and selling of real property.
He has been real estate advisor
to KFWB (980AM) radio.*

MICHAEL D. HILLER

REAL ESTATE BROKER - LAWYER

REAL ESTATE BROKER
SINCE 1959

LAWYER
SINCE 1962

HILLER REALTY
16055 VENTURA BLVD., SUITE 603   ENCINO, CA 91436   (818) 990-7843

PLEASE SIGN, OBTAIN OTHER SIGNATURES, AND RETURN THIS PETITION TO SHOW OUR STRENGTH IN OBTAINING REMEDIAL REAL ESTATE LOAN LEGISLATION

PETITION FOR NOTE MODIFICATION AGREEMENTS

I'm tired of being ripped off for excessive and unnecessary real estate loan fees!!!

I am a real estate property owner in California.

I will support, vote, and work for legislation and/or a BALLOT INITIATIVE to force financial institutions to charge only a reasonable loan fee percentage("points") for a new loan which does not increase my original Note secured by Deed of Trust with the same lender who is offering the same interest rate to the general public.

I will pay the loan fee from my own funds and thus need only a NOTE MODIFICATION AGREEMENT which can be processed in 1 HOUR rather than 4 months!

No more appraisal fees, credit check/report fees, escrow fees nor title insurance--since I will have a lower monthly payment and the original Deed of Trust remains on record with its remaining term of years. My credit is better than before with a new and lower payment; the appraisal is unnecessary since no new loan funds are sought; and escrow unnecessary without funds being processed.

NAME _____ ADDRESS _____ PHONE _____

_____

_____

_____

_____

_____

_____

_____

_____

_____

_____